The
Shanghai
I Knew

Ellis Jacob

COMTEQ™
PUBLISHING
MARGATE, NEW JERSEY

Published by:
    ComteQ Publishing
    A division of ComteQ Communications, LLC
    P.O. Box 3046
    Margate, New Jersey 08402
    609-487-9000 • Fax 609-822-4098
    Email: publisher@ComteQcom.com
    Website: www.ComteQpublishing.com

ISBN10 0-9793771-0-2
ISBN13 978-0-9793771-0-5
Library of Congress Control Number: 2007922809

Book and cover design by Rob Huberman

Printed in the United States of America
10 9 8 7 6 5 4 3 2 1

This book is dedicated to my children, Cynthia, David and Lisa, who survived my pilgrimage back to my roots in Shanghai, and to all those people who lived in Shanghai during the tumultuous days before, during and immediately after World War II. They experienced the history of Shanghai during those days

Table of Contents

Acknowledgements

This book would not have been possible without the assistance and contributions of many people. Those people contributed, suggested, assisted, edited, critiqued, commented on, or participated in the writing and formulation of the book in some way.

The first to come to mind is my second cousin Rose Jacob Horowitz, whose production of the Jacob family tree proved to be most invaluable. Her comments and notes and references of our lives in Shanghai were an additional bonus. I also received assistance in the form of historical and reference material from Michael Orapello, a fine friend and high school classmate of mine, who lent me a considerable amount of material in the form of magazine articles about Shanghai, and who, on his own, performed many internet searches, providing me with much background material of Shanghai, the origins of the American Marines in Shanghai, and commentary on my early writings. Thanks to Mickey, I received a steady stream of information relating to assorted aspects of life in Shanghai, historical perspectives of Shanghai and of China. This, of course, prodded me into working on the manuscript further, when I was inclined to put it away for a while. Dick Kask, another friend and high school classmate provided a most unusual lift to my book, by lending me a set of scrapbooks put together by his father, in which there were clippings of photographs, articles and pages of the North China Daily News, during the 1937 Japanese invasion of Shanghai, showing the battles between the Japanese Imperial forces and the Chinese defending the villages around the city.

Many of my cousins stepped up with tidbits, anecdotes, and tales of their experiences while growing up as I did. Emma Levy Wachtin helped with material about the Shanghai Jewish School. Katie Levy Fox told about her experiences with local currencies and the wild inflation we survived. Rahma Levy Thomas was immensely helpful in providing material about the Chinese currencies and the exchange rates for the changes in currencies, and provided much useful information on the early Chinese currencies. Leah Jacob Garrick provided many helpful comments, and the anecdotes about her life in the western part of the city and experiences with the servants. My uncle Solomon Jacob helped with stories about his grandfather's manservant, and information about his father.

My friend Charlie Stock told about his experiences with the exclusion of Chinese from certain parts of the city, and also the effects of inflation. Bobbie Tchakalian, a former classmate of mine, also mentioned the restrictions against Chinese from certain parts of the city. Mayna Avent Nance, a schoolmate of mine, provided me with a menu from a restaurant illustrating the effects of inflation.

Milt Simpson, a good friend of mine, who was a graphic designer and experienced in the production of many books, provided me with invaluable information relating to the design, features, details and quality of a book. He was also a great source of information concerning the Jewish communities and in particular some Jewish persons residing in Shanghai concurrent with my stay there. He provided me with lots of information sources from the internet, and helped enrich the book immensely.

Les Faulkner, whom I knew while at AT&T, performed a superb job of editing the manuscript, instilling a sense of action to the manuscript, changing it from a rather passive document to one of movement and activity.   Werner Simon performed further editing while removing some ambivalent statements.   He also provided concise wording to many sentences, eliminating much of my sloppy writing.   Finally, my dear friend Helen Lippman provided invaluable assistance, with comments and commentary, moral support, and by proofing the document.

Many authors of books on Shanghai proved to be extremely helpful in providing a picture and background of one of the most interesting cities in the world, with a unique past and an extremely bright future.   Some authors, whose books are listed in the Bibliography include Stella Dong, Bernard Wasserstein, Gregory Patent, George Wang and Betty Barr, Maisie Meyer and Sigmund Tobias.

Preface

Early in 1987, I decided to go back and visit Shanghai, China, where I was born and raised until I was 18 years old. My childhood and adolescence witnessed the tremendous political upheavals and government changes that took place in the years before, during and immediately after World War II. These tumultuous times were profoundly unsettling to the inhabitants of the city, disturbing their serenity and changing the conditions under which they lived. However, my fond memories of growing up in such an environment compelled me to return to review a part of the world that is unique in its history, culture and architecture.

My three children, Cynthia, David and Lisa, and a friend, Kathy Win, accompanied me. Kathy was a valuable asset to our trip. She spoke fluent Mandarin, the universal dialect of China, and served as our interpreter and our translator during much of the trip. We visited Beijing, Xian and finally, Shanghai. We saw the Great Wall, the Ming Tombs, the Forbidden City, Tien An Men Square in Beijing; the terra cotta warriors and the hot springs spa in Xian. Of course we visited all my old haunts in Shanghai, and some attractions I hadn't seen when I was living there, such as the Jade Pagoda and the Arts and Crafts Museum, where some of the handiwork is of incredibly good quality.

My visit to Shanghai was emotional. It brought back many memories, not all of them pleasant. However, all of them helped shape me into the person I became. The city was pretty much as I remembered it, and I knew my way around even though I hadn't been there in 38 years. We would rent a taxi for 8 hours, and I could direct the driver through the city to wherever I wished to go. I would see a house, or the door of a house, that would jolt my memory. I would see the dome or the wall of a building, and suddenly some memory would overtake me. We stayed in the Shanghai Hotel, two blocks from the mansion of the Nissim families. The sight of the mansion flooded my head with memories, bringing tears dangerously close. I experienced this many times while traveling around the city.

It was during this trip and shortly afterward that the seed for a book found its way into my mind. For some time it stayed there, simmering and slowly taking shape in my consciousness. Even so, I remember thinking that I was going to write about my experiences someday. Then, one day, I remember saying to myself, "Stop fooling yourself, you're either going to do it now, or you're not going to do it at all." It took about two years of gathering materials, photographs, notes, and talking and interviewing people, before I would start. The result is what follows.

I decided to write my personal history of growing up in Shanghai, not only because I would present a different facet of life there; since the horrific events of September 11, 2001, we in the United States have had a disturbing feeling of insecurity. We thought it could not happen to us here, but it did. We also thought that even if something did happen here, it probably couldn't happen again. But it can. For those of us who lived in the International Settlement of Shanghai (a section of the city governed by an international governing body), and in the other parts of the city, there was considerable insecurity. But life went on, and for the inhabitants some semblance of normalcy prevailed. Those of us who stayed for any length of time strove to establish at least a façade of normalcy and permanence. In the end, it became clear that the sense of security comes from within.

Let me provide you with an idea of the constant undermining of security: In 8 years, from 1941 to 1949, inhabitants of Shanghai lived under four consecutive and very different governments, each with its own police force and a distinct currency. At first there was a constant threat of incursions by Japanese Imperial forces, then occupation by the Japanese, followed by bombing by American planes, wild inflation, liberation by Chinese Nationalist and American forces, and then occupation or 'liberation' again, by the Peoples' Liberation Army. At times, inflation was so great that no one dealt in the local currency for significant amounts of money or time. One would figure out what the cost of doing business or buying something in terms of the U.S. dollar or the British pound sterling, or even the Chinese silver dollar, and then business would be transacted on that basis.

During all this turmoil, life proceeded as normally as it could, with some long periods of serenity. People grew up in or came to Shanghai, lived there, were educated there, married, produced families, and conducted themselves as they would have in their own respective countries, maintaining customs and values they had brought with them.

However, the society that the 'foreigners' (non-Chinese) lived in was basically a privileged and parasitic society, in many ways demeaning to the Chinese populace. In the International Settlement where I lived, the government was strongly British influenced, and English was the primary language. One did not need to speak or know Chinese to manage there. Chinese people, except for wealthy Chinese, were the sub-class, performing all the heavy and menial work that required little or no education. They were the servants, domestics, cooks, chauffeurs, and laborers. The government of the International Settlement just before World War II consisted of representatives of many Western nations. This government was the Shanghai Municipal Council. There were no Chinese representatives in the Shanghai Municipal Council until 1930, much to the frustration of the Chinese. However, a Chinese City Council was established that administered to the many Chinese inhabited areas in the environs of Shanghai. In the

International Settlement there were separate facilities for Chinese and for foreigners: schools were separate, sports facilities were separate, some parts of the city were not open to Chinese, and there were many places that Chinese were allowed in only as guests or as employees. This situation lasted until the international areas were returned to China, in principle in 1943, during World War II, and in actuality immediately following the war.

The history of Shanghai is unique. It became a prominent locale, thanks to the treaties that ended two wars fought over the English rights to sell opium to China. It was also recognized for its strategic location near the mouth of the Yangtze River, on one of its tributaries. Shanghai is near the coast, about halfway between the northern and southern ends of the Chinese coastline, and at a convergence of railway lines. Its relative proximity to many other important locations such as Nanking, Peking, Hong Kong, Tokyo, the Philippines, and other points in the Far East was a bonus.

It was in this environment that I grew up. While there was some sense of insecurity after the Japanese attacked China in 1932 and again in 1937, I was too young to notice it. As time went on the insecurity became more apparent, especially since the foreign population lived so far away from the western countries from which the many inhabitants originated. And even then we went about our business as though nothing really mattered regarding the threats to our way of life. Then, earth-shaking events took place, upsetting our equilibrium, changing the status of our existences forever, and we adjusted to the new situation each time. When the Communists overran Shanghai in 1949, they started encouraging foreigners to leave. This is when my family and I left Shanghai. We set sail for Canada by way of the United States.

In the years just before World War II, Shanghai was known as a haven for refugees from Europe, because the city did not require a passport or visa to enter. One needed only to pay for passage to Shanghai to get away from the strife that was plaguing other parts of the world. This was in sharp contrast to the long lines at embassies and consulates of many western countries, where people were trying to escape the Nazi madness, mostly to no avail. The

United States stopped issuing visas to German and Austrian citizens; they didn't want too many Jews coming to their shores. And the Swiss heavily guarded their borders to prevent Jews from getting across from Germany and Austria. It was difficult to get visas to other European countries as well. Some Jews had the misfortune to emigrate to Belgium, only to be caught there when the Germans overran the country in 1940. So Shanghai stood out like a beacon from a lighthouse, where no visa was required, only payment of passage and perhaps payment to the border guards or Gestapo agents at the borders.

This story is written mainly from my memories of my life in Shanghai, with a little help from my friends, with consultations and conversations with relatives, and lots of help from the many fine books and documents regarding the conditions and incidents that took place there. The origins of the materials from outside sources are referenced and duly noted. The accuracy of the events and my experiences discussed in this book have been checked with documents and periodicals whenever possible. Discussions and interviews were held with relatives, associates, classmates and friends to ensure that those events and experiences are recalled as accurately as possible. Street names used here are those of prewar Shanghai, the British and French names. I have included these in a map of Shanghai, as well as a brief history of Shanghai and a brief background of my family.

I have written the book of my life in a historical context, giving brief descriptions of events and their impacts on my life as they occurred. There are names of people that appear only once. These were people who entered my life, and then left, because their families were recalled back to their home countries, or they left for because of unsettling political or military conditions. There were many people who had some small but memorable impact on my life.

In writing my personal history, I have included the correct names of people I have encountered, except in the few instances in which the narrative or anecdote would cause embarrassment or reflect negatively upon them. In those cases I have changed the

names of the people involved. Only in rare instances were any
names changed. It is not my intention for this book to be a
sensational, tell all, expose. When referring to any foods or
incidents or titles, I have used the Sephardic terms and spellings,
transliterating if necessary. I was privileged to have been born and
raised in an environment and at a time that was unique, raised in
an ancient culture, Jewish, and in constant contact with another
ancient culture, Chinese, while having been brought up in a
predominantly British and western community. That, to my mind,
is a most unusual combination.

The Shanghai that I have observed and described in this book
no longer exists. It was mostly a colonial era society, a remnant of
western outreach into the Far East. The International Settlement
was mostly western dominated, with western architecture, western
institutions and customs, with English spoken predominantly
during interactions between westerners and between westerners
and Chinese. Chinese was spoken only when necessary, in the
instances that the Chinese person could not speak English. As a
result, pidgin English developed, with words like mahski (never
mind, or, it's all right) and walla walla (noise, ado, fuss).

Several good books have been written about Shanghai in this
era. Many of these are listed in the bibliography and referred to in
the notes at the end of this book, or quoted with due attribution in
the text itself. While my references to Shanghai mean the
International Settlement and the French Concession, there were
many attached villages surrounding these areas, populated by
Chinese in much more densely packed neighborhoods. These
included Nantao, Chapei, Yangtzepoo, Pootung and many others.
The book that comes to mind immediately is *Shanghai Boy,
Shanghai Girl, Lives in Parallel*, by George Wang and Betty Barr, a
book that I highly recommend. It brings into focus the glaring
privileged world of westerners, and the vast difference in living
standards and comforts between the foreign and Chinese
communities. I must point out that my life was in parallel with the
two writers of that book. In fact, I was born in between their birth
dates, and my life was in proximity to Betty Barr's. I went to the

school in the Western extension of Shanghai, and was in the boys' school at the time Betty was in the girls' school. The two schools were adjacent to each other. After World War II, we were classmates at the Shanghai American School. We graduated together a few days after the communist takeover of Shanghai. Upon comparison of our lives, it is clear that the parasitic society in which westerners lived could not endure and was sure to come to an abrupt end, especially with the end of colonialism and the growth of Chinese nationalism.

This book is intended to record life, scenery, incidents and observations of a colorful era in the most colorful city in the Far East, if not the world. It is by no means complete, and probably leaves out much; this will be for someone else to fill in. It is only the observations and experiences of one fortunate to have grown up in a society that in so many ways was unusual and unique, and has long since passed into history. It is written from the point of view of a young boy and then a teenager growing up in that environment, with all his perspectives and prejudices. Many details of life and conditions during this period are not included, simply because of my lack of awareness of those conditions. For those details, I recommend many of the fine books written about life in Shanghai listed in the bibliography. Shanghai has moved beyond those days and those ways, as the world has. Only the reminiscences remain. But the experiences have influenced many lives, given an unusual perspective, and provided for many interesting conversations.

And so I present the memoirs of a Shanghailander, or Old China Hand, as the case may be, from the eyes of an Iraqi Jew from China, educated in British and American schools, (and a short stint in a Jewish school), raised in a western society that was cosmopolitan and colonial, strongly influenced by British standards and customs, and yet also influenced and enriched by contact with the Chinese society and customs. I am most thankful for Shanghai's contribution to the richness of my life.

Chapter One
BEGINNINGS

s I was growing up in Shanghai in the 1930s, I was amazed at the diversity of its population. How is it, I thought, that I am part of such a wide and varying group of people? Where did we all come from? How did my family get to Shanghai? It took me a long time to find the answers to these questions.

Although I grew up in a Sephardic Jewish family of middle-eastern origins in a Chinese city, I spoke neither Hebrew, Arabic, nor Chinese. I spoke English as all my peers and relatives did. But I did learn to speak a little Chinese as I grew up, and I learned some Arabic at home from listening to my parents and family. Also, at an early age I learned enough Hebrew to be able to recite the prayers in the synagogue, and improved further when I studied for my Bar Miswah.

In the compound in front of our apartment building, I remember playing with a Danish boy, a Swedish boy, some Americans, the Wildt brothers, a couple of Italian boys, an Irish boy by the name of Paddy Sweeny, a Portuguese boy, some Russians, many Jewish boys, and an English boy by the name of Kenneth Toon, who was my age and became a classmate of mine. Of course, there were some girls playing in the compound too.

There was Dora Vidumsky who lived down the lane, Sally Goldenberg who lived in the Garden Apartments around the corner from us, and many other girls whose names I no longer remember.

I soon became aware of the large family to which I belonged, because of the size of the family activities. I had lots of cousins on both my parents' sides, and many uncles and aunts. My second cousin, Rose Jacob Horowitz, was the one who told me about our beginnings and our odyssey from western Asia to the Far East.

Both my parents' families originated in Iraq. My father's family lived in the area surrounding Baghdad and the town of Anah near the Syrian border. His mother's family came from Basra. Both families and the communities in which they lived, were strict orthodox Jews. Saleh, cousin Rose's father and my father's uncle, told Rose that, "Although they say we are Baghdadi (from Baghdad), we are really Babli (from Babylon)." This means that our family originated in ancient Babylon, where Jews were sent after the destruction of the First Temple, some two hundred years before the Christian era.

In Hebrew, "ben" means "son of." In the Jewish culture, it was common for a boy to be called his given name, son of his father's name. My great grandfather was Isaiah, son of Jacob. During the Ottoman Empire era in the 19th century, Jews who originally had just one name took on their fathers' names as their surnames. My great grandfather, Isaiah ben Jacob, became Isaiah Jacob, and thus the Jacob clan began.

In the 1800's there were Jewish communities in many Iraqi towns, and although the Jewish populations had lived in those towns for many generations, there was always some sense of insecurity. This insecurity was well justified by events that took place in those towns.

My paternal grandfather, Jacob Shalom Jacob, was educated in a French missionary school in Baghdad, Ecole Alliance Israelite Universelle. There, of course, he learned to read and write. In 1886, his younger brother, my granduncle Saleh, was 7 years old when he was caught in an anti-Jewish riot around Passover time.

This happened in Baghdad. He was in a suq, (a bazaar with many small stalls and winding, narrow paths.) He was hit by rocks, and left unconscious and bleeding on the street. Luckily, someone recognized him and carried him to his mother, my great grandmother, who nursed him back to health.

My great grandmother, widowed and with several children to raise and protect, decided that the family needed to leave for its own safety. The family was ultimately put in contact with the Sassoons of India.

David Sassoon made his fortune dealing in opium, and he invested his money wisely. He had manufacturing and real estate interests in India, as well as shipping and other commercial interests. In the 1880s, all records were handled manually. There were no office machines, typewriters, calculators, or computers; everything was done by hand. And so he would hire anyone who could read and write, especially Jewish applicants. David Sassoon offered my grandfather a job immediately, and Jacob Shalom Jacob moved to Bombay, India. The family followed him shortly afterward.

Thus the Jacob family's fortunes centered on life in Bombay, and fared quite well while there, from the early 1880s until the turn of the century. My granduncle Saleh, the younger brother of my grandfather, was sent to the David Sassoon School in Bombay. As a teenager, he supervised the weighing of cotton bales for an Austrian Jewish cotton merchant. This merchant liked Saleh so much that he took Saleh into his home for 3 years to teach his sons pre-Bar Miswah Hebrew and prayers. After that, Saleh went to work in the bookkeeping department of David Sassoon & Company.

Around the turn of the century, my grandfather was transferred to Shanghai, where he went to work for David Sassoon & Company managing their real estate interests. My grandfather told his sons that while the Sassoons were shipping opium to China at an enormous profit, David Sassoon offered my grandfather an opportunity to invest in a shipment of opium, with the potential of making huge profits for himself. My grandfather refused.

Shanghai was a Treaty Port, one of many in China where western nations had secured rights for their citizens and business interests. Westerners were immune from Chinese law and instead were subject to the laws of their home countries. The rights were obtained in grossly unequal treaties signed with the government of China. Shanghai, particularly, was well-situated, and western nations were showing great interest in the city for its commercial potential. Real estate was growing at a phenomenal rate.

In 1902 my grandfather met a 15-year-old Iraqi Jewish girl, Aziza Abraham. She had recently arrived with her father and family from Basra, Iraq. Her father, Sassoon Abraham, was the Hazzan and Shohet to the small but growing Sephardic Jewish community in Shanghai. (A Hazzan conducts the prayers in the synagogue and a Shohet is the person who performs the prayers and the ritual slaying of chickens and cows to conform to kosher law). I don't remember my great grandfather Abraham; he passed away when I was very young, but it was after him that I was given my middle name.

Sassoon Abraham was a wonderful, caring man who always had a smile and a good word for everyone. As he was the Hazzan, he wanted to welcome newcomers to Shanghai. He had two servants, a married Chinese couple. The manservant, Khooncha, learned to speak fluent Arabic, and was familiar with Sephardic and orthodox Jewish customs. At that time there were many people arriving from the Middle East, especially from Iraq. Sassoon Abraham would send Khooncha to the docks to greet newcomers. A Middle Eastern newcomer was easily identifiable because he usually wore a fez and was often darker-complexioned than other immigrants. This Chinese man would approach the person and astound him by speaking to him in fluent Arabic, a warm welcome indeed to the Sephardic community in Shanghai.

In 1903, Jacob Shalom Jacob and Aziza Abraham were wed the year after they met, in an arranged marriage, conducted in the British Consulate. Their marriage certificate is shown on page 131. They produced 10 children, nine boys and a girl. Of the ten children, my father, Joseph Raymond Jacob, was the second child.

The first child, his older brother, was Isaiah Jacob. Early in the lives of the children, scarlet fever ran through the family, affecting many of the children. One son, Ezekiel, died of the disease; the daughter, my aunt Hilda, was brain damaged and remained at the mental age of 12 for the rest of her life. My father and my uncle Isaiah had kidney trouble most of their lives. The family grew up in a house on Boone Road and later moved to Carter Road in Shanghai until some of the sons married and moved out of the household. The remaining family members moved to an apartment off Yu Yuen Road where my grandfather passed away. My widowed grandmother and her unmarried sons then moved into a large apartment in the Garden Apartment complex on Bubbling Well Road, just off Seymour Road.

I would visit my grandmother after school sometimes, and we would have tea and cake in the afternoons. She was the matriarch, and would send her children scurrying about with orders like, "Bring me some water," or "Make me some tea," and of course, whichever son was so commanded would dutifully perform the task. This took place although she had servants, who didn't seem to be around at those times. Granny, as I called her, always treated me with great warmth, and called me Sonny Boy.

My grandmother was a feminist long before feminism was popular or acceptable. She spoke Arabic fluently, and knew the culture and customs of the Middle East. She understood that the area she came from was a male-dominated one, to which she objected strongly. In Arabic, "Ibn" means "son of" and "Abu" means "father of." But there were no corresponding words for "daughter of" and "mother of." One day, when I was visiting my grandmother, she was angry, very angry. I asked her, "Granny, why are you so angry?" In broken English, she said to me, "Why they say 'son of' and 'father of'? Why they don't say 'daughter of' and 'mother of'? You know why? I tell you why. Because they have balls, that's why!" I was nine or ten years old, and I was terribly embarrassed by her outburst. She said it many times, to many people, to express her anger at the male-centered culture.

In addition to the Jacob branch emanating from my

grandfather, there were two other Jacob branches of the family. My grandfather's brother, Ezra, and his wife, Sophie, produced seven children, and my grandfather's younger brother, Saleh, and his wife, Miriam, produced two children, one of whom is cousin Rose, whom you have already met.

My mother's family, the Levys, left Basra, Iraq, for India. My mother's parents had two sons while in Iraq, George and Aaron Levy, both born in Basra. They then moved to Calcutta, India, where they brought two more children into the world, aunt Regina and my mother. Because the daughters were born in India, known as the British Raj—the pearl of the British Empire—they were officially British subjects. Their mother either died giving birth to my mother, or she died soon after my mother's birth. And so her father, my grandfather, whom I knew only as Abooyee, raised 4 children on his own. It is not clear when the Levy daughters were actually born. In the 1920s they wanted to go to the United States, and being too young, they lied about their ages, changing the years of their births. My mother and aunt Regina left for Shanghai with their father some time before World War I, circa 1914 to 1918. A photo of my mother and aunt Regina is shown on page 132.

The two Levy sons married young Iraqi girls and began raising families. My uncle George married 14-year-old Sophie Azair, who was born in Basra, in an arranged marriage. In 1934, they emigrated to Shanghai.

My uncle, Aaron (actually named Aharon Shaul Nissim Levy) married Rachel Elias in 1926. She was born in Bombay, India. My aunt Regina married John Goldenberg in 1922. Uncle John was born in Alexandria, Egypt, of Romanian Jewish parents. Early in his life he attended college in Jerusalem. The family moved to the Far East in 1914, early in the First World War. The ship on which they sailed had to undergo blackouts at night due to the presence of a German battleship in the Indian Ocean threatening all British shipping in the area. Uncle John had a brother, Bill, and a sister, Lisa.

My parents met in Shanghai and were married on July 2, 1930. A photo of their wedding is shown on page 133.

We lived in a Sephardic Jewish community, which at its peak numbered around 1,000. It was not a ghetto in which the citizens are concentrated in a small area. The members of this community lived mainly in the International Settlement, north of Bubbling Well Road, toward the western part of the city. Many lived in the western addition of the city, west of St. George's Square. You could identify most of us by our family names—everyone had a biblical name of some sort. In addition to the Jacob clan that I described above, there were three other Jacob families, unrelated to us. One Jacob family lived on Seymour Road. The father in the family became the Hazzan of the Ohel Rachel Synagogue when I was young. I remember him conducting the prayers in the synagogue. One of the sons in this family was also named Ellis Jacob. I remember that the family was warm and friendly. A second Jacob family also lived on Seymour Road, at the foot of the lane leading to the Cosmopolitan Apartments. The third Jacob family lived in the western extension of the city, and they originated in Iran (Persia in those days). I don't know much about that family, except that some of them attended the synagogue on the occasions that I was there.

There were communities of many other nationalities established in Shanghai. Besides the Sephardic Jewish community, there was an Ashkenazi Jewish community, mainly from Russia. Many of these members made the long trek by train across Siberia to Vladivostok and Harbin and then to Shanghai. They came after the Russo-Japanese war of 1904, and after the Russian Revolution in 1917 and the civil war that followed, from 1917 to 1920. Most of the Russian Jews attended an Ashkenazi Synagogue in the French Concession. Unfortunately, there was little interaction between the two Jewish communities in Shanghai. The only interactions between the Ashkenazi and Sephardic Jews were among the children, in the Shanghai Jewish School. The Ashkenazi population in Shanghai reached about 3,000 at its peak.

Of course, there were many other communities: American, French, British, Italian, German, Portuguese, Swiss, and Russian. The latter consisted mostly of White Russians who had fled after the Russian Revolution and during the civil war that followed. These people were strongly anti-communist, but there was a small Soviet community too. The Portuguese community was large enough to establish and support a community center called the Lusitano Club. Most of the Portuguese came from Macao, a Portuguese island colony near Hong Kong, and many were Eurasians.

The prominent German community had its own school in Shanghai. The German population had both pro-Nazi and non-Nazi Germans, and physical violence sometimes erupted between them. Albert Hess, with whom I attended school after the war, had scars as a result of some beatings from his Nazi persecutors.

The American community was mostly composed of missionaries, merchants, and military personnel. It was large enough to support the Shanghai American School, originally located in the northern part of the city, and then in the French Concession on Avenue Petain in the late 1920s. Before the move, the school was known as the American School in Shanghai, and when they competed with other schools, they were teased by their opponents' calls of "ASS." They soon changed the name of the school to the Shanghai American School and so the initials SAS were born.

The English-speaking community as a whole supported many schools and institutions in the city. In all cases, people lived among others of different nationalities, interspersed with each other. There were also Chinese, some who were very wealthy. The International Settlement and the French Concession were a hodgepodge of people from mainly western countries, surrounded by villages which were inhabited almost totally by Chinese in densely overcrowded conditions.

In the mid-1930s, with the Nazis in total control of Germany and menacing Central Europe, they began a vicious persecution of Jews. Shanghai then experienced a strong influx of Jewish refugees from Central and Eastern Europe. When many other countries and cities closed their doors to the thousands of Jews fleeing the Nazi madness, many Jews looked to Shanghai as a haven for survival.

There were no passport or visa requirements. The British did not want to provide the Japanese with passport or visa authority because there was a Japanese representative on the Shanghai Municipal Council. As a result, refugees flocked to Shanghai in large numbers. There were no welfare protections like we have today, such as food stamps and subsidized housing for the poor, unemployment insurance, and health benefits for those unable to pay for them. It goes without saying that the two Jewish communities established in Shanghai at the time, with a combined population of 4,000, were overwhelmed by the appearance of some 20,000 refugees. Most did not speak English, many had spent all their savings to reach Shanghai, and none brought any furniture or belongings other than their clothing and personal effects. Many of the Sephardic Jews, with some help from the Ashkenazi community, strove to find housing, clothing, food, schooling and employment for the new arrivals. It was an overwhelming and daunting task, made possible with the help of the affluent Sephardic Jews such as the Hardoons, the Kadoories, the Abrahams, and many others. American Jewish relief agencies also helped to get the new refugees settled and fed. As might be expected, there was an extreme culture shock for those Europeans when they arrived. Most of the new arrivals were housed in run-down buildings and apartments in Hongkew, the Japanese part of the city where such buildings were readily available, many of which had no western toilets.

I soon came into contact with kids of all ages of many different nationalities in school, in the YMCA, in the sports fields (there were no playgrounds as we know them), and everywhere in the city. The common feature in our lives was that we all spoke English. But then what about Shanghai? How did the city become this way?

Shanghai has a most unusual history. Since early times, Shanghai had a significant population presence on the banks of the Whangpoo River. A settlement at the Shanghai location was said to have existed since about the 11th century of the Christian Era. Many merchants lived in Shanghai who traded in cotton, rice and other commodities, and the small community flourished. A wall was built around the city in the 16th century to protect it from marauding pirates. In 1840, Shanghai was a fishing village. There was some small industry, but little of great significance. There was also a small foreign presence. Shanghai's location was recognized early for its strategic value for commerce, transportation and communication. As a result of the two wars fought by the British against the Chinese for the right to sell opium to China, grossly uneven treaties were signed, the first in 1842, giving western powers certain rights in several ports, called Treaty Ports. These rights were called Extra Territoriality rights, or extrality for short. These rights mandated that citizens of certain western nations were not subject to Chinese laws and regulations in those ports. Laws, regulations and taxes were dispensed by the western powers, and their citizens were subject to the laws of their home countries. Thus, the International Settlement of Shanghai was born. This international section was located 2 miles north of the walled city, and had little to do with the Chinese part of the city.

In 1843, after the first Opium War, the British were given the concession north of the existing Chinese city and south of the Soochow Creek. They built buildings along the river front, on what was *The Bund*[1] (rhymes with fund), and city grew westward from there.

After the second Opium War, around 1849, other western powers demanded and received concessions. The American settlement was north of the Soochow Creek, and with the other powers' concessions, the entire area became the International Settlement. The French balked and demanded their own concession and were given the area between the International Settlement and the Chinese walled city. Shanghai grew quickly, mostly because it provided convenient access to the Chinese markets, especially opium.

The growth rate accelerated after 1853, as a result of the threat of the Taiping Rebellion (beginning in 1848), when refugees flocked into the city and were no longer barred from living within the boundaries of the International Settlement. Chinese were allowed to live in the International Settlement after that. With the influx of those refugees into the foreign part of the city, real estate prices soared, providing huge profits to those with the ability to build cheap houses on any piece of land that could be gotten. In the 1860s even faster growth occurred because of the Taiping threat, and Shanghai became the fastest growing city in the world, faster than San Francisco during the gold rush days, and probably with the fastest growth rate of any city in history. To provide you with an idea of the growth rate, it was estimated that in 1840, the population of Shanghai was about 6,000. In 1940, Shanghai was a thriving metropolis with a population of 6 million. Thus in 100 years, Shanghai grew in population by 1,000 times.

The Shanghai Municipal Council was created in 1863 to govern the International and American parts of the city. It consisted of representatives from Japan and eight western nations. No Chinese representatives sat on the Shanghai Municipal Council for decades, much to the frustration and consternation of the Chinese, who could only vote for representatives on the Council as *foreign* rate-payers.

There was a Chinese governing body, called the Shanghai City Council, which governed the Chinese areas of the city with oversight from the Central Government, that consisted of the many villages and districts adjacent to the international parts of the city. In addition to the International Settlement, the French government demanded and received a concession governed by the French Consul. It was called the French Concession and was adjacent to and just south of the International Settlement.

All streets in the French Concession were named after French heroes, such as Avenue Petain, Avenue Foch, Rue Cardinal Mercier, and so on. Just north of the Soochow Creek was the American district, which was soon combined with the International sector to form the International Settlement, and northeast of that was an area called Hongkew, which was controlled by the Japanese. This area was known as Little Tokyo, where Japanese inhabitants lived, conducted their business and entertained themselves and rarely ventured outside the area. Foreigners would go into the district to enjoy sukiyaki, and drink sake and Japanese beer in a typical Japanese setting.

Many Shanghai street names were in English, often to commemorate prominent English men or English icons, and had names like Seymour Road, Connaught Road, and St. George's Square. However, a great many of the streets downtown were named after cities and provinces of China, such as Nanking Road, Foochow Road, and Szechuan Road, always with anglicized versions of the Chinese names. Then there were streets with purely Chinese names, such as Tifeng Road and Yu Yuen Road. In the business area, the streets leading east-west were named after Chinese cities, and those leading north-south were named after provinces.

The most famous street in Shanghai, and probably in all of Asia, was The Bund, which ran along the river. The Bund's stately, western-styled buildings housed the large banks, consulates and hotels, presenting a majestic vista to those seeing Shanghai for the first time. The Long Bar at the Shanghai Club, also on The Bund, was over 100 feet long, reputed to be the longest bar in the world.

As Shanghai grew, it became increasingly westernized and anglicized. Lavish clubs and opulent restaurants were constructed. Wide streets appeared in the residential parts of the city toward the west of the business district. Luxurious mansions were built with innumerable rooms, managed by an army of servants. But as the city's business stature grew, so did the low-life. Brothels multiplied in large numbers, catering to the many seamen who went ashore as shipping expanded.

Shanghai soon developed a reputation as a place of degeneracy, of evil and crime. It became a magnet for criminals of all sorts, from many parts of the world. An American missionary, upon reviewing the state of societal decay, once said, "If Shanghai survives, then God owes an apology to Sodom and Gomorrah." The term "Shanghaied" meant to be taken aboard ship in a drugged or unconscious state and forced to sail away from the port from which one was so incapacitated, or forced to perform duties against one's will. Depending on one's point of view, Shanghai was the

Paris of the East, the Pearl of the Orient, or the Whore of Asia. It turns out all those monikers were well deserved.

In the 1880s many missionaries ventured to Shanghai hoping to save the souls of the heathens. It was these missionaries who clamored for decency and morality in the city. Nevertheless, the brothels proliferated.

The city was a magnet for Chinese from all parts of the country. As described by Stella Dong in her excellent book *SHANGHAI The Rise and Fall of a Decadent City,* "First had come the Cantonese accompanying the foreign traders north; then the Ningponese, whose merchants and bankers brought their entrepreneurial prowess to Shanghai commerce and industry; then gentry from Hangchow, Soochow, Wusih, and the other wealthy cities of southern Kiangsu, who joined forces with the Ningponese to dominate the Chinese business world; and finally, and most numerous of all, wave after wave of peasants from northern Kiangsu, Shantung, Anwhei, Hupeh, and other provinces who provided the great port with an enormous and always replenishable labor force." And so Shanghai became a mixture of Chinese from all over China, especially the coastal, central and northern provinces, and with them came all the dialects, customs, perspectives and attitudes.

But with the great influx of Chinese, there came a newly found sense of freedom and free thought. As many of the Chinese went abroad to study and returned with ideas of equality and democracy, criticisms of the Ching dynasty grew. Shanghai became the most progressive, forward-looking of all Chinese cities and has continued to be so until the present day.

In the early 1900s, Shanghai was a hotbed of revolutionary activities. Many secret societies were born there in the first two decades of the 20th century. Sun Yat-Sen and his revolutionary groups were active in Shanghai, and Sun Yat-Sen visited the city many times. Chiang Kai-Shek, the Generalissimo as he liked to be called and the future President of the Nationalist Government of China, got his start in leadership there, and had a house in the French Concession. Chou En-Lai, the future Prime Minister of the

32

32

Ellis Jacob

Peoples' Republic of China, was also a strong presence, and had to go underground when a price was put on his head. Chiang Ching, who became the wife of Mao Tse-Tung, got her start as an actress in Shanghai. Ho Chi Minh, the future leader of a united Vietnam, lived and worked in Shanghai and stayed at the YMCA for a time, under the very noses of the French authorities while they were looking for him

In 1917 the British government prohibited the export of opium from India to China, and then in 1918 the Chinese government in Peking banned the trafficking and use of opium. This caused opium traffic to go underground, and similar to what prohibition did to the consumption of alcohol in the United States, opium use flourished.

In 1919, an International Gun Embargo brought a large number of gun dealers to Shanghai, with boatloads of weapons of all kinds. These dealers sold to anyone interested in their wares. They lived extravagantly, wheeling and dealing in the best hotels in the city. At this time, Shanghai was known as a safe haven for criminals of all kinds, and they came from all over the world.

Despite strong institutions like banking, places of worship, and expansive areas of legitimate business, the Shanghai of the 1920s saw great opium trading. In fact, there was a large ship moored in the Whangpoo River that was used as a storage facility for opium, and from which opium was delivered to its destination. The 1920s also saw many battles between various warlords in and around Shanghai, damaging surrounding villages and causing considerable human suffering. Many refugees flocked to Shanghai, especially into the French Concession. The warlords had large armies and engaged in kidnapping for ransom, extortion and looting. They had their own territories, and turf battles waged on.

One of the secret societies was the Green Gang, a group of gangsters involved in extortion, opium importing and distribution and other nefarious activities. Huang Jin-Rong was head of the Green Gang, and controlled much of the racketeering activity, especially in the French Concession. In fact, the French Consul, in order to keep the crime rate at an acceptable level, appointed

Huang Jin-Rong Police Chief in the French Concession. The French authorities looked the other way as long as the crimes were kept mainly away from the foreign population. Since Huang had power over the criminal activities *and* the police, he was able to solve many crimes by calling on his gang to return stolen property, or to capture many petty criminals, much to the delight of the authorities.

Meantime, a young, ambitious thug by the name of Tu Yueh-Sen worked his way up the criminal ladder and soon controlled the opium traffic in the French Concession. He monopolized the traffic of opium there, not only controlling its flow, but getting a kickback for every ounce of opium sold in the area. After Huang was kidnapped by a rival gang, and subsequently released thanks to Tu Yueh-Sen, his loss of face caused a great loss of prestige and power, which then went to Tu Yueh-Sen. Tu became known as the Master of Shanghai, and ruled from his position ruthlessly and violently.

As a result of the great trade in arms taking place because of the International Arms Embargo, Shanghai saw a sharp increase in crimes, especially robberies and kidnapping. Criminal organizations set up in one municipality would conduct their activities in another municipality and thus avoid prosecution there. If one municipality clamped down on their criminal activities, they would simply move to another. Shanghai was really three municipalities adjacent to each other, each with a different governing authority, and so it was easy to move from one location to the next, because there were no physical barriers separating the different municipalities. This mobility was rampant in opium dens, gambling dens and any other racketeering activity. Many gambling dens, when raided, simply paid their fines and continued to operate, or would shut down and move across the street or a block away, across the border to the next town. During this time Shanghai's well-publicized nightlife flourished. Dance halls and nightclubs sprung up like mushrooms after a rain. The famous Del Monte's was located in the Chinese part of the city, and so was out of reach of the western authorities.

During the early 1920s there was a huge migration of White Russians as a result of their defeat at the hands of the Bolsheviks. These were hard times for White Russians. Many of their skills were unwanted or of no use to the new environs. Some men joined the police force or joined the Shanghai Volunteer Corps (SVC) to utilize their military skills. The women joined the dance halls and danced for tickets and a share of drinks they could entice their dance partners to buy. Or they joined the many brothels about the city. With this great influx, even more brothels sprang up, and some well-appointed bordellos.

Unrest continued in Shanghai, especially in the Chinese parts of the city, where factories, mills, warehouses and businesses employed large numbers of Chinese workers. These workers labored under appalling conditions, for very poor wages, and with little or no protection from their bosses. As a result, communist ideas proliferated and some took hold among the workers. Chou En-Lai was active in Shanghai at this time, organizing cells, stirring workers to protest and spreading the communist doctrines. In 1925, as a result of the strong communist activity, laborers demonstrated against their working conditions and pay. The protest was broken up with firearms, and 11 demonstrators were killed. This was followed by an anti-foreign demonstration on May 30, 1925. In June an extensive walk off and general strike immobilized Shanghai, shutting down industrial activity, municipal services, utilities, dockyards, even the press. Taking Shanghai's lead, strikes and demonstrations spread to many Chinese cities. Large numbers of demonstrators were killed, and this became known as the May 30th Movement. Hong Kong was crippled for over a year. In many cities mobs stormed the British Consulates and forced a return of the concessions in those cities. Western inhabitants feared this would happen in Shanghai, and imported 40,000 troops to protect their citizens and interests. Nevertheless, the city was again shut down in 1926.

In the meantime, revolutionaries had formed the Kuomingtang Party (Kuomingtang means "Keep the nation together"), and Sun Yat-Sen became the leader of the new Republic. This movement was betrayed by General Yuan Shi-Kai, who wanted to establish himself as the new emperor of China. He failed in this attempt, and died soon afterward. The country disintegrated into areas controlled by warlords. Chiang Kai-Shek rose up the ranks of the Kuomingtang Party, and took control of its army in the south. Moving northward, he systematically eliminated many of the warlords. During this time, the Communists supported the Kuomingtang. Chiang Kai-Shek consolidated his leadership and power in the party, and in a betrayal of the Communists, drove them out of the party. This occurred in a particularly bloody time in Shanghai, in 1927. A workers' strike in Shanghai seriously hurt the economy and productivity of the Chinese factories. With the help of Tu Yueh-Sen, Green Gang members went into the Chinese districts north of the International Settlement, and in conjunction with Kuomingtang agents, massacred thousands of trade unionists and workers. It is no wonder Tu Yueh-Sen was called the Al Capone of the Orient.

Despite the mayhem caused by workers' agitation and the consequences of those, and as incongruous as it could be, Chiang Kai-Shek married Soong Mei-Ling in 1927 at the Majestic Hotel, in a most lavish wedding, and anyone who was anyone in Shanghai was invited to the wedding.

It was feared that Chiang Kai-Shek would then move on to Shanghai to reclaim the return of the concessions from the western powers, but other issues dominated his attention, namely his attack and attempted elimination of the Communists. As a result, the Chinese Communist Party, which was formed by a congress in Shanghai in 1921, went underground.

A period of relative labor calm then befell Shanghai, but in 1931 and 1932, China was rocked by an invasion of Japanese Imperial forces. In 1931, after creating an incident the Japanese army occupied Manchuria, in the north of China, making it a province of Japan and calling it Manchukuo. But with patriotic fervor running high in Shanghai, a Japanese boycott was organized there, and very effectively shut down all Japanese enterprises in the city. Chinese merchants caught with Japanese goods were insulted and sworn at. Chinese laborers refused to unload Japanese ships, and Japanese factories were closed. This conflict gave the Japanese naval commander an excuse to expand Japanese interests in Shanghai. The Japanese Consul made demands of the Chinese authorities (among them, an end to the boycott of Japanese goods and factories). The Japanese Naval Commander, Admiral Shiozawa, did not wait for a reply and attacked Chapei and the North Railway Station. Chapei was bombed and shelled, but the Chinese army there put up heroic resistance. Finally a truce was signed by the two sides, with most of the Japanese troops leaving Shanghai, and the Chinese army having to vacate an area around Shanghai, creating a demilitarized zone.

Shanghai was a center of great intrigue at this time. Communist agents formed numerous cells, which gave rise to spy rings in many parts of the world. One such ring operated in Tokyo before and during World War II, even into the German embassy there. Another was active in Oxford. In fact, Shanghai became the Red General Headquarters of Asia, coordinating revolutionary activities and movements in Asia.

This was the Shanghai that I knew, a Shanghai that had long ago lost its innocence, racked by workers' struggles for better treatment and working conditions. It was a city of three municipalities with strong international business interests protected by an international military force, with glaring inequalities in treatment and living standards between foreigners and Chinese. It was a city of great privilege and luxurious lifestyles for many foreigners, and great extremes of wealth and poverty. By this time Shanghai had become the fifth largest city in the world and accounted for about half of the import/export trade of all China, and was the most prominent city in the Far East. Most large corporations in the world had branches in Shanghai. Shanghai was easily as modern as any city in the world. Art Deco buildings, lavish building lobbies, and furnishings abounded. Clothing styles reflected the best in western styles. The telephone system was as modern as those of New York or London. Our family did not have a party line telephone, and I don't know anyone who did.

Shanghai was really a European city planted in China, with adjacent villages densely populated by Chinese surrounding the European sections. The architecture was for the most part European. The Bund along the Whangpoo River was easily the most famous street in all of Asia and was the pride of the Europeans. The British Consulate stood on the northernmost point on The Bund, next to the Soochow creek and the Garden Bridge that crossed it. And as you traveled south along The Bund, you would see majestic buildings housing the many banks and other businesses, giving The Bund its European flavor. The Hong Kong and Shanghai Banking Corporation was in one of the buildings, guarded by a pair of larger-than-life bronze lions. The Cathay Hotel and the Palace Hotel stood on each side of the beginning of Nanking Road, on The Bund.

There were buildings housing the great shipping company of Jardine Matheson & Company, the North China Daily News, a great variety of banks, the Custom House, and the Shanghai Club with its long bar and exclusive membership, the latter marking the southern end of The Bund and the end of the International Settlement, and the beginning of the French Concession. A continuation southward along the street which was then called the Quai de France would show a great mass of commercial activity with godowns (warehouses) and docks, and assorted but less imposing buildings, until one reached the walled-in, original Shanghai called Nantao.

This was Shanghai's Chinatown. Shanghai was known as the only city in China with its own Chinatown. The Whangpoo River bustled with an enormous amount of shipping activity. There were steamships from foreign lands, many *sampans*[2], and Chinese junks[3]. Flowing into the Whangpoo River was the Soochow Creek at the north end of the International Settlement. Floating in the Soochow Creek were rows and rows of sampans tied together where a great variety of goods and foods could be purchased and where masses of people lived. Some people spent their entire lives on these sampans; they slept, raised families and entertained themselves, never needing to leave the sampans. To say that the

Soochow Creek was contaminated was an understatement, since all the refuse from the sampans was discarded into the Creek.

This was Shanghai in the early 1930's, a modern, westernized city governed by an international council, which had no Chinese representatives and was predominantly British in nature and culture, and one in which Chinese had very few rights, adjacent to a French Concession governed by a French Consul but also westernized, with French street names and mostly western architecture, which had more tolerance for borderline legal activities. These areas were surrounded on three sides by many villages and districts densely inhabited by Chinese and governed by a Chinese Shanghai City Council. The police forces exhibited interesting differences. The police of the International Settlement were composed of Sikhs from India and individuals from many western nations, such as Russia and Great Britain. The higher officers were mostly British ex-soldiers hired after World War I.

The next tier were the Russians. Having left their homeland, many of the Russians had difficulty starting anew. However, with the military experiences and skills, many were hired locally and filled a great need in the police force. The Sikhs were mainly the traffic police, and in the lowest tier were the Chinese constables. The police in the French Concession consisted of French, Chinese, and members of the French Indo-Chinese colonies, such as Annamese. The officers were French, and their subordinates were Asian. The police in the Chinese areas were strictly Chinese. Across the river from the three districts was Pootung, an area of godowns and industrial properties, dockyards and farmland.

I was to learn all about the origins of my family and the history of Shanghai much later, when I was no longer living in Shanghai.

Chapter Two
Early Life In Shanghai

I was born in the Country Hospital in Shanghai on July 29, 1931. My birth certificate with the name Elias Sassoon Jacob on it, was issued by the Jewish Communal Association of Shanghai. I have no idea how Elias became Ellis, but I have been Ellis as far back as I can remember. My Hebrew name is Eliyahu Sasson Ya'akob, and when anglicized is Elijah Sassoon Jacob. The Sassoon was named after my great grandfather, Sassoon Abraham, the father of my paternal grandmother. I don't know for whom I was given the name Elias.

Page 134 shows me at about 3 years old. At this age, I used to lie across my mother's lap while she gently rubbed my back. It was most comforting. There was usually family around when this occurred, uncles and aunts, which added a deep feeling of security. This feeling was to remain with me for much of my life in Shanghai, even though events took place that would tend to undermine my security. Thanks to the extensive families on both my father's and mother's sides, I felt secure during the most formative years of my life.

One of my earliest memories is of an apartment building being built that was owned by my grandfather. A picture on page 135 shows the Jacob clan, taken on the roof of the building after its completion. I was younger than five then, and my parents would take me to the apartment building while it was being built. Building materials were strewn on the floors, on the ground, everywhere. Isaiah Elias, a wonderful, kind family friend who was involved in the construction of the building, took me around the building, giving me some spare tiles to play with. They were square and hexagonal tiles adhering to paper backing, to be used in kitchens and bathrooms, and Isaiah gave me some to take home. I was delighted. I peeled them off the paper and played with them, making playhouses, and anything else that came to my imagination.

My next recollection of growing up in Shanghai is when I was about five years old. I was in the back yard of a house, with a small wall around it. There were bushes around the edges, at the base of the walls, probably rose bushes. The back yard was small, about 30 feet by 40 feet, and covered with grass. There was room for me and other children my age to run about. There were lots of grownups looking intently at a chess or backgammon board (we called them towli, rhyming with wow-lee). I believe this was my father's parents' home on Carter Road.

This was around the mid-1930s and these were happy times. There was lots of company and attention and many children to play with.

It was comforting to know that our relatives lived all around us and close by. My mother's sister, Aunt Regina, lived with her husband, my uncle John Goldenberg, and two children, Jackie and Katie, in an apartment directly above us. My uncle George Levy, who was married to my aunt Sophie, lived with their children, Mike, Katie, Emma, and Albert, around the corner on Bubbling Well Road. A photo of my uncle George and aunt Sophie is shown on page 132. My mother's next oldest brother, my uncle Aaron Levy lived with his wife, aunt Rachel, and their children, Rahma, Hannah, Hazel, Ruth, Kittie, Joe, and Bennie, in a house on a lane behind us, off Bubbling Well Road. My mother's father, whom I knew as Abooyee, lived in a room on the top floor of the house inhabited by my uncle Aaron Levy and family. A picture of Abooyee is shown on page 132.

My father's parents had lived in an apartment off Yu Yuen Road, but after my grandfather died, my grandmother moved into an apartment around the corner on Bubbling Well Road in the Garden Apartments. She lived there with her unmarried children, my uncles, Moses, Aaron, Ellis and Solomon, all Jacobs. My father had three other brothers: Isaiah, who lived on Yu Yuen Road with my aunt Becky and their three children, Leah, Rachel and Jackie; his younger brother, David, and his wife Aziza, who also lived on Yu Yuen Road with their children, Daniel, Lenny and Shelley; and his immediate younger brother, Isaac, whom I hadn't met, but who had gone to England to study, and about whom the family always spoke with great pride. Uncle Isaac, after serving in the military during World War II, went on to become the Queen's Master, and the top judge on the High Court in England. He was knighted, and known as Sir Jack (for Jacob). I vaguely remember my grandfather, my father's father. He had a white beard, and always seemed to have a skullcap on. He died in 1936 when I was about 5 years old, and so I don't remember him well. Almost all the Jacob uncles and aunts and all the Jacob cousins were born in Shanghai.

On the Jacob side of the family, there were always family gatherings for the many religious holidays and social occasions. For Pesah (Passover) and Rosh Hashanah (New Year), my parents and I would go to my grandmother's place, where my father's brothers and their families would be also, and we would celebrate these times as one big family. I can remember one Rosh Hashanah at my grandmother's, with the family gathered together, when I was about seven or eight years old. My four-year-old cousin Daniel was whining and carrying on. My grandmother went over to him and asked, "Danny Boy, what's the matter?" And he said, "I can't find my ball." With that, she reached for the front of his pants and said, "But you have a ball!" Everyone had a good laugh at that, but I was very embarrassed.

For Succoth, we went to my uncle Isaiah's and aunt Becky's place, where they had made a succah, or an autumn enclosure with no roof overhead, to celebrate the harvest festival Succoth, with singing and lots of good food.

There was no observance or celebration of Christmas. Instead, at about the same time, we observed Hannukah, although this was not considered a major holiday. I don't even remember if we lit candles during the holiday to commemorate the eight days of the holiday. While we didn't in our home, in many of my uncles' homes candles were lit to commemorate the holiday. We certainly did not receive any presents.

Pesah with the Jacobs' was the most memorable. The Jacob family got together, with all the uncles and aunts and their children. The younger generation, my cousins and I, each had a piece of *matzos* (we called it *mussah*) wrapped in a bandana and tied over our shoulders with the *matzos* on our backs. At some point during the evening, all the cousins left the room and closed the door behind us. Then the oldest of us knocked on the door, and a voice called out "Who are you?" We answered, "We are the children of Israel." The voice then called out, "Where are you coming from?" And we would answer, "From Egypt." "And where are you going?" the voice called out and we said, "To the land of Canaan." Then came, "What do you want?" And we came in singing, *"Ma nish ta nah..."* and had a wonderful dinner. The *matzos* that we had was quite unlike machine-made *matzos* available in the United States. Our matzos was made by hand in a clay oven. The *matzos* came out round and brittle and about a foot in diameter and most resembles today's cracker bread.

Since I was young at the time, my friends and I used to play games with walnuts, in which we would try to knock the opponent's walnuts out of a circle and get to keep them. In another game, a line was drawn in the dirt, and we would compete with each other by rolling walnuts toward the line. The one closest to the line won and took all the other walnuts. I never won at those games, and would lose lots of walnuts.

We celebrated the festival of Purim, (we pronounced it pooREEM). This was a joyous festival, in which Jewish communities celebrated the preserving of the Jews in Persia in ancient times, when Esther convinced the Persian king Ahasuerus (the Greeks called him Xerxes) to spare the Jews against the plan of his advisor, the hated Haman, to destroy the Jews. It appears that Mordecai, cousin of the Queen Esther, aroused the enmity of Haman, the Prime Minister, who then induced the king to issue an edict to destroy the Jews. Haman and his henchmen would cast lots to determine the time the Jews were to be annihilated. But Queen Esther interceded, and convinced the king to reverse the edict, and to condemn Haman and his followers instead.

Purim comes from the Persian word *Pur*, meaning casting of lots, which implied luck or fate. The Sephardic community celebrated by gambling in many forms, mostly card games. While the adults would play serious gambling games, the children would pay Black Jack for fun. We called the game by its French name, *vingt et un*.

All my male Jacob cousins were known by their first names with boy added to it. Danny Boy's younger brother Lenny was known as Lenny Boy. My cousin Jackie was known as Jackie Boy. And for some reason, the family called me Sonny, and so I was Sonny Boy.

There were so many Jacob brothers that, together with their Jacob cousins, they formed a football (soccer) team. The Jacobs played with other teams from the Sephardic community. It was the Jacobs against the rest. The Jacobs were pretty good football players, but many of them wore glasses, and if it rained they would lose, because they often had to stop to wipe off their lenses.

My grandfather did well for his family. He invested in real estate, and at one time owned three apartment buildings. The one on Route Dufour was opened when I was quite young and was the one to which my parents took me as it was being built. The whole family went to the apartment and posed for the photograph on the roof of the building, shown in the photograph on page 135.

On Saturday nights, we sometimes went to my uncle Aaron and aunt Rachel Levy's place for dinner. I enjoyed those evenings enormously. Instead of our normal dinner fare, we had what we called a "light dinner," which usually consisted of toast and cheese and jams. It was the cheese I remember most. We had white cheese, what we would call farmer's cheese today. It was very salty, and could not be eaten plain. Instead, slices of the cheese would be put into a bowl of warm water for a few minutes, to flush out most of the saltiness, and then the cheese would be eaten on toast or bread, or crackers. The cheese by that time would be soft and chewy, and had a subtle, pleasing flavor. Some of the jams were homemade and delicious. Plum jam was made by first removing the pits, and then adding water to them in a large pot and then boiling them into a thick jam. It was sweet but tart and most flavorful. It was then that I learned that cheese and jam made a great combination—a blend of sweet and salty tastes—which I relish to this day.

On occasion we visited my aunt Sophie and uncle George Levy. I always felt my aunt Sophie's cooking was in a class by itself. She made a great variety of middle-eastern dishes, including Arabian curry, sambuseks, which were meat turnovers that were fried and crunchy, or cheese turnovers that were baked, —all gourmet delights. The meat sambuseks are similar to South American turnovers known as empanadas, with the crusts lighter and crispier.

I was cared for by a Chinese maid, an amah, whom I remember with great fondness. She had a warm, sincere smile and a pleasant personality. She fed, bathed and clothed me when I was very young, but also had a family of her own. Her husband who would appear regularly and stay with her and then would disappear off and on, to the country where I think his parents had a small farm, and where, I found out later, he had a girlfriend. But then he would appear once again and all would be well with her family. My amah and her husband had a daughter, Mary, a year older than me, a son, Li Chuen, a year younger than me and another son, Ah Fook, 3 years younger than me. I never knew my amah's name, or her husband's. I knew her simply as "Amah." Sometimes in the evenings I would eat with them, at their table in the back of our apartment. Their food was really delicious—even better than ours! They had a bean paste, much like miso, that one would collect on a chopstick, and then spread on rice to be eaten with whatever food that would go on the rice, or on the food itself. It added a wonderful flavor to the food. I'm thankful that I interacted with their family a lot, and learned some of their customs. As Chinese New Year approached, the family would prepare for a feast, and I looked forward to that. But more importantly, the Chinese had a custom of paying off debts at New Year's, literally or symbolically. And so at New Year's, my amah and her husband would give to their children, and also to me, some coins wrapped in red paper, as a symbol of paying off their debts. I always liked this custom and looked forward to it each year.

My family's apartment was on the first floor, which was the first floor above street level. The apartment consisted of a large living room with a small verandah, a hall leading to a good-sized bedroom, and to a bathroom off the hall. My bed was in the corner of my parents' bedroom. Another hall from the living room led to the front door and to the pantry and kitchen, which were small by current standards. Off the kitchen was a small back verandah, and at the other end of that was a small room in which the amah and her family lived. This room was no more that 6 feet by 12 feet without windows, but the amah's entire family lived in it!

Our apartment had a coal-burning stove in the living room with the stove pipe and chimney leading out of one of the living room windows. The winters were quite cold, and when there was a wind, it was bitterly cold. Conversely, summers were hot and muggy, although there were still many pleasant days to enjoy.

In the summer we slept under mosquito nets, and we burned coils of fragrant-smelling mosquito repellent. This aroma had a soporific effect on me and helped me to fall asleep each night.

We had a cook, who learned to prepare western food. He cooked not only things like cutlets, and stews, but also the Arabian food on which our family was raised. He prepared cabbage, and peppers or tomatoes that were stuffed with ground meat and many Arabian spices. We called these dishes mahushah. He made other Arabian dishes with delightful sauces that we would have over rice. Since we didn't have access to the kind of vegetables normally used for such dishes, he would improvise and use locally found vegetables, and included some locally found nuts as well. He made what we called potato chops, which were mashed potatoes stuffed with cooked meat and spices, and then breaded and fried. One dish in particular was most memorable. It was called mahmoosah, which consisted of diced cooked potatoes, onions, parsley or cilantro, eggs and many spices like turmeric or cumin, all lightly fried. This is similar to a Spanish dish called torta, which is made of finely chopped onions lightly fried in advance, added to chopped potatoes, eggs, salt and pepper. This was all fried, turned over and fried again. It is one of the items for Tapas, the late afternoon snack that the Spanish enjoy. At the Sunday noon meal our cook prepared a Chinese meal for us.

My father was not religious, but my mother observed the many Jewish traditions and kept a kosher home. The only indication that ours was a Jewish household was the mezuzah on the door frame of the front door to our apartment. We had a closet that was locked throughout the year, except for just before Passover, when it was opened and the Passover dishes, pots and pans were brought out. They were cleaned and made ready for use during the Passover holidays. After the Passover observance, they were washed and put back into the closet, which was locked for another year.

We lived in the Cosmopolitan Apartments, located on the old Seymour Road, about a half block off Bubbling Well Road, now called Nanjing Lu. When I was growing up those streets were called Seemoh Lu (Seymour Road) and Jing Ansi Lu respectively, by the Chinese. The Cosmopolitan Apartments consisted of a main building, seven stories high, with two satellite buildings of three stories each, one each to the north and south of the main building. We lived in the north building.

My aunt Regina and uncle John and family lived directly above us on the second floor. Their children, Jackie and Katie, used to fight with each other, and I was jealous because I was an only child and had no one to fight with. Jackie used the back room of their apartment. The wall between the back room and the rest of the apartment was removed so that he had access to the apartment without having to go around the back. Above them lived a Portuguese family, a mother, her sister and her son. The son, we'll call Alfonso, was a year or so older than me, and I used to go up to their apartment to play when I was about 6 years old. He had lots of toy soldiers, with uniforms of various countries, and we would have many wars on the floor of his room. In the corner near where we played there was an altar with a statue of Mary on it, and on the wall was Jesus on a cross. One day, I clearly remember Alfonso's mother warning me to never turn my back on the statues, because, she said, "If you do, you will die." That made a tremendous impression on me. Some time later, as we were playing on the floor, I found myself with my back to the altar, and I whipped around as fast as I could, almost scared to death. From then on, I made sure that whenever I was in that room, I always faced the altar.

The apartment buildings were set back from the street about 100 yards, connected to it by two lanes on which there were little two-story houses. In front of the main building there was a small courtyard and park, and parking spaces for a few cars. In front of the side buildings were walkways leading to the side buildings and small grassy areas where children could play. The apartments and houses on the lanes were inhabited mostly by families of foreign (non-Chinese) descent, and a few Chinese who could afford them. The children would play in the courtyard. I played with many kids from the complex, all of them foreigners. We did not play with Chinese children. In fact, I don't ever remember seeing Chinese children playing in the lanes or in the park.

While staying at the Cosmopolitan, my amah would take me up to the roof of our apartment building, just above the third floor. The roof covered the entire building, so we children had a lot of room to play. One day when I was 6 years old, I was running about on the roof with some other children when we heard the drone of airplanes, many of them, and then two loud explosions. I was very frightened, and my amah immediately took me downstairs into our apartment. Years later, I found out that those planes were Japanese (or Chinese) bombers. They had attacked a heavily populated intersection on Avenue Edouard VII, and there were many civilian casualties. Japanese planes also bombed an area on Nanking Road, near the Bund. This was the beginning of the second Japanese aggression against China, during which the Japanese occupied the many Chinese villages surrounding Shanghai and the Chinese parts of Shanghai.

Japan invaded North China in 1932 and occupied Manchuria, which they annexed and called Manchukuo. However, Japan had greater designs for the area, and after a couple of incidents which Japan used as pretexts, the last one occurring on July 7, 1937, Japan conducted a full-fledged invasion of China. Japanese forces quickly occupied Beijing and many towns and cities in North China, then landed and attacked Shanghai on August 13, 1937, and invaded South China as well. In Shanghai, the Japanese cruiser *Idzumo* sailed up the Whangpoo River, and thousands of Japanese troops landed in the area.

The Japanese plan was to occupy most of China in 3 months. But the Chinese put up stiff resistance, especially in and around Shanghai. Chinese troops were not as well-armed and didn't have the heavy-gun support that the Japanese had, and so were eventually driven out of the area, but not without a great fight and fierce and heroic resistance. In Chapei, where much of the fighting took place, the Chinese burnt much of the town before retreating, depriving the Japanese from taking the town undamaged. The Japanese cruiser *Idzumo* shelled Pootung, opposite Shanghai, causing great damage and many fires.

The Chinese repeatedly tried to hit the cruiser with no success. Chinese planes tried to bomb the *Idzumo*, and Chinese patrol boats tried to torpedo the ship, but all missed. This took place in the areas surrounding the International Settlement and French Concession of Shanghai. Japanese planes dropped bombs on an intersection in the internationally controlled area which was heavily populated, causing great loss of life. These were the bombs that I heard the day I was playing on the roof. There were huge fires and tremendous destruction in the villages and areas surrounding the International Settlement and French Concession, which could be seen from the rooftops and streets.

Western nations sent troops and warships to Shanghai to protect their citizens and interests, and evacuations of many westerners took place. British women and children were evacuated to Hong Kong. The U.S. 4th Marine Regiment was already stationed in Shanghai, and the 6th Marine Regiment arrived to augment the American presence. British troops were also stationed in Shanghai. The Italian government sent their Savoy Grenadier Regiment, and the French had regular army troops, supported by Indo-Chinese units. The USS *Augusta* sailed up the Whangpoo River, as did warships of many other nations. Amazingly, life went on in the international areas as though nothing had happened. Polo games took place. There were dances, concerts, sports activities, school functions, all while explosions and fires were heard and seen around the city!

After the Japanese completely occupied the Chinese parts of Shanghai they advanced inland and attacked Nanking, leading to the "Rape of Nanking"[4]. But after the Japanese drove out the Chinese troops, all was calm in Shanghai. The Japanese occupied much of North China, the coastal provinces and up the Yangtze River to Nanking for the duration of the war until 1945. They set up a puppet Chinese government in Nanking under the leadership of Wang Ching-Wei in March, 1940, and the Nationalist government of Chiang Kai-Shek moved its headquarters to Chunking. Wang Ching-Wei was not highly regarded by most Chinese. They considered him a traitor, and he was assassinated toward the end of World War II.

Even during these troubling times, though, my parents had an active social life. My father belonged to a bridge club, where he played at least two evenings a week. My mother had a mahjong circle, and also played during the week. So as I was growing up, I was frequently alone on weeknights because the amah stayed in her room with her family. I was afraid that my parents were never coming home, and I would often cry myself to sleep. The next morning when I awoke, there were my parents and all was well again. On the weekends my parents frequently attended parties, and so I was left alone again. But sometimes my cousin Katie came down to watch me and slept in the room with me.

She was five years older than I was, but we had a nice relationship: a connection that lasts until this day. She was the sister I never had. On other occasions, when I made a loud enough fuss, my amah's daughter came to stay with me. She was a year older than I was and I welcomed her company. Even so, I developed an insecurity that stayed with me for some time afterward.

My parents were both employed full time. My father worked in an office downtown that handled imports and exports, and my mother was a stenographer for Wheelock and Company. My father sometimes came home for lunch, which we called *tiffin*[5]. Sometimes he had his *tiffins* out and returned home soon after. He had a nap for about a half hour, and then went back to his office at around 2:00 p.m. Work during the second half of the day lasted until early evening, then he began his evening activities, a game of bridge or squash. He would sometimes come home at about 7 or 8:00 in the evening or later for dinner. Very often, though, he would be out for the evening, and if my mother had a *mahjong* game somewhere, I would have dinner alone.

My father spoke Shanghai dialect Chinese fluently, and more than once he told me that it was a shame that we didn't learn more about Chinese customs and culture. He was kind and understanding toward the Chinese with whom he interacted. In his office there were three Chinese employees, and on the occasions that I went to his office, I noticed that he treated them well and with respect.

He had many dealings with members of the foreign community, and in his dealings, much of it was conducted verbally. He told me about an expression called "Putee Book," which meant that a particular transaction was agreed upon and could be put in the book. Many business transactions were concluded with nothing more than a handshake. Such transactions, he told me, could only be conducted with the British or those of the British Commonwealth countries but when you conducted business with Americans, everything had to be in writing. I was disappointed to hear that.

One time, we found that our cook and perhaps our amah had been helping themselves to some of the food that was kept in our pantry. Cooking oil was kept in a large tin can, and there were many canned products also stored there. One day my mother found much of the oil and canned products missing. She was quite upset, and of course suspicion fell on the servants. My father told both servants that he didn't like them stealing, but that if they wanted or needed some of the food we had, to please ask for it, and they could have it. He told my mother and me he was aware of their relative poverty and that he was sensitive to their needs. The problem never arose again. The servants got their cooking oil and assorted other food whenever they needed it.

My uncle Isaiah Jacob and his family had similar but more humorous experiences. He noticed that the whiskey in his liquor cabinet was getting lighter in color and the whiskey itself tasted weaker. He couldn't understand why, although he had his suspicions. The whiskey itself began to taste weaker and weaker as time went on. He suspected that the servants were helping themselves to the liquor, and replacing the amount they had taken with water, making the liquor lighter in color.

This could not be proved, until an amusing incident took place. He had a bottle of arak, an anisette-flavored, middle eastern liquor that is quite strong and clear and colorless. (Arak is known in the Mediterranean area as Ouzo or Raki). However, when this liquor is mixed with water, it becomes cream colored. Soon after the bottle of arak was opened, it suddenly became cream-colored, a clear indication that someone had added water to it to replace the missing liquor.

I don't remember having many toys. In fact I'm not sure I had any toys at all, except for a locally adapted *Monopoly* game, called Shanghai Millionaire. Instead of street names of Atlantic City, the game had street names from Shanghai. The most expensive street was The Bund, instead of Boardwalk.

I did have books, although not many were children's books. During my childhood, I liked the ones with lots of pictures in them. My father had a bookcase filled to the ceiling with books, and was an avid reader. As I grew up, my father got me interested in an author by the name of Rafael Sabatini, who wrote historical novels. I still treasure the Sabatini books that I have from my younger days—The *Sea Hawk*, *Scaramouche* and *Captain Blood*. And when I went to see Errol Flynn in *Captain Blood*, it had much more meaning for me.

When I was a child, my parents often took me to the Nissims' house, a mansion on the corner of Tifeng and Great Western Roads. It was a two-story building with a large yard, and a smaller building at the other end of the yard with a Chinese kiosk, where many kids would play. The entire property was surrounded by a wall, so that there was privacy in the back yard and within the building. Two Nissim families lived in the house. They were related by the fathers, who were brothers, Maani and Nouri Nissim. Maani Nissim and his wife Flora had 3 sons, Matty, Shulie and Sammy. Noori Nissim and his wife Nazira had a son, Albert, and 2 daughters, Rachel and Mona.

And so, when I went to the Nissims' I would play with Albert and Rachel, who were about my age. Albert and Rachel's amah was a pleasant woman who had bound feet about the size of small hands, and she hobbled about slowly, with her feet in tiny Chinese shoes. But the most memorable person was the grandmother, Maani's and Nouri's mother. She was a live wire. She challenged anyone and everyone to play towli, and would usually beat them. She had a perpetual smile and a great sense of humor, but she ruled her family; she was its matriarch.

Also during those early years, I spent a weekend now and then at my granduncle Saleh's and auntie Bobbie's place on Yu Yuen Road. Their two children, Joe (we called him Joe Joe), and Rosie, were older than I was. But the whole family made me feel welcome and were so good to me. I delighted in having breakfast with uncle Saleh and auntie Bobbie—they made me feel so special!

I went to kindergarten, which was located in the western part of the city. Since we were living in a strongly British-influenced society, the school was a very British school, called the Western District Public School. (A public school by British standards is a private school). There were actually two schools, side by side, separated by a fence, both located on Yu Yuen Road, slightly west of Tifeng Road. On the corner of Tifeng Road and YuYuen Road was a firehouse, which is still there today. Adjacent to that firehouse and to the west were the two schools. The one next to the firehouse was the boys' school, and the one beyond it was the girls' school. The schools were run by the Shanghai Municipal Council for foreign children. They also ran schools for Chinese children. In the British education system, boys and girls were together in kindergarten, but after that boys went to the boys' school, and girls went to the girls' school. And so my amah took me to kindergarten, located in the girls' school, which was to be my only taste of coeducation for a number of years. The kindergarten was in a large room, in which chairs were set against the walls. The teacher sat in the middle of the room and taught, although I don't remember what she taught us. We didn't have coloring books, construction paper, desks, tables or anything one would expect in kindergarten these days.

So after kindergarten, I went to the boys' school. Grades were called forms. Instead of first grade or second grade, it was form one and form two, respectively. Although my memory is hazy about much of the early grades, I do remember some of the later grades and some of the teachers in those grades. At around form six, we had a physics teacher by the name of Mr. Pyle. He was a soft-spoken, gentle man, who tried to instill some appreciation for elementary physics. He also taught us mathematics, giving us a solid foundation, which helped me in my subsequent schooling.

Another teacher who made a lasting impression on me was Mrs. Hepburn. She was very attractive, with blond hair combed straight back. She almost always wore a leopard skin coat over her shoulders. She never smiled, and always had a stern look on her face. She taught us English and Writing, and dictated sentences for us to write, then critiqued us on the quality of our writing. She walked up and down the rows of desks with a stick in her hand. If any of us was caught writing left-handed, we were whacked across the knuckles.

As luck would have it, I was left-handed, so I was whacked across the knuckles a few times. But I learned fast, and as she approached, I would switch to my right hand. Out on the playground, we teased each other by saying, "The right hand is the right hand. The left hand is the wrong hand!" Although Mrs. Hepburn could easily determine by the quality of my handwriting when I was writing with my left hand and when with my right, she never said anything if she didn't catch me. She had a terrible disposition, and I was quite afraid of her. If a student asked a question she didn't think was appropriate, she would responded loudly, "The impudence and boldness of you!" and would sometimes send a boy down to the headmaster, Mr. Bennett, for little or no reason. I was deathly afraid of Mr. Bennett. He was a gray-haired, energetic man, who would wander through the halls ensuring that everything was in order. He used to cane students who were sent to him, so I made sure I wasn't sent down to his office.

Mr. Bennett used to apply the term "fee waster" to any of the boys sent to his office. Parents of the boys going to the school had to pay a fee to send their children to the school. So he meant that we were wasting our parents' fees. Fortunately, I was never called a fee waster. Mr. Bennett once mentioned to my grandmother that because she had so many of her sons attend the Western District Public School, her family paid the highest fees of anyone.

We learned English history and English geography, and while I can picture the face of that teacher, I cannot remember his name. But the irony of it is that we learned more about the British Isles than we did about China, the country we were living in! We learned about the knights and their armor, and the lines of English kings, and of course about Henry the 8th, who had six wives in succession. But not a thing about China!

And then there was Mr. Tingle. Billy Tingle. Mr. Tingle taught gym. He was a short, stocky man, who was a boxer at one time. He coached us in soccer, and he was good at it, giving us good tips and training on strategy and tactics on the field. But his forte was boxing. Most often we would be in the gym, and he would guide us on the fine points of boxing. There would be a mat in the middle of the floor, and Mr. Tingle would spend a few minutes on some of the things to learn about boxing, and then he would say, "You and you," pointing to 2 of the boys in the class. The boys would put on gloves and box for 3 minutes, with Mr. Tingle giving them a critique at the end. Then he would say, "You and you," pointing to two other boys, and so on.

From my perspective, the most distinct aspect of gym class was that whenever I was one of the "yous," the other "you" was Ronnie Martin. Ronnie Martin was my age, but he was at least three inches taller than I was, weighed about 30 pounds more than I did, and had an arm's reach three inches longer than mine. So when Ronnie and I got on the mat, I was his punching bag for three minutes. Once, instead of having boxing, we had wrestling. And, sure enough, I was on the mat with Ronnie Martin. There was no way I could match him with brawn, so I had to outsmart him. I leaned forward like I was going to lunge at him, and he dove at me. When he did, I stepped aside and he went flat on the mat.

I clearly remember Mr. Tingle with his veddy veddy British accent, saying, "Oh, you mustn't let him fool you!" I can remember thinking, "Whose side is he on? And why is he on anyone's side?" Well, with Ronnie Martin on the mat, I dove at him, and tried to pin him. But I was no match for him, and it ended with him pinning me to the mat. But I gave it a good try. Years later, at a reunion in San Francisco with many of us who attended the British schools in Shanghai, I was told that Mr. Tingle didn't like Jewish boys and would think of ways to punish them. Then I remembered all the beatings I took at the hands of Ronnie Martin.

But those were happy days at the Western District Public School. I was in Form 1 through Form 6 at the school, aged 6 to 12. When I was about 8 years old, I was given money to take the tram to school. To get to the tram, I had to walk over three blocks to the north, to Avenue Road, and catch the tram to St. George's Square, where the trams turned around. Often I would simply walk up Bubbling Well Road, west to St. George's Square, a distance of less than one mile, and keep the money. St. George's

Square was one long block east of Yu Yuen Road and Tifeng Road, where the school was.

Our primary mode of travel was the rickshaw, a two-wheel vehicle seating one or two people, with a pair of arms stretching forward from the seats and joined at the front. Between those arms, the rickshaw coolie raised the rickshaw and balanced it so that he could just run, and not have to lift the weight of the passengers. Those rickshaw coolies could travel great distances, and had great stamina. They would frequently have only straw sandals on their feet and run in them all day. The rickshaw also had a top that could be pulled up over the passengers in case of rain, somewhat like the top of a convertible car, only smaller and simpler. During the rain the rickshaw coolie would also put up a covering at the front of the top cover to prevent rain from coming into the sheltered area.

In the early 1940s the pedicab appeared. This was a 3-wheeler and had a pair of handlebars over the front wheel for steering, a seat just behind the handlebars, and pedals with a chain reaching to the back axle that drove the vehicle. It also had the pull up covering and tarp in case of rain. Because it traveled much faster than the rickshaw, it became the preferred mode of travel. There were trams that conveyed passengers all the way to the river, from St. George's Square and other places. One of the tram lines went up and down Avenue Road. The tram driver stepped on a pedal that made a "dinging" sound as he made his way down the road. The tram speed was controlled by a lever that had several settings, and was about waist high to the driver.

Some people, particularly the wealthy ones, had cars. But Shanghai was not that large a city that one could not walk to most places. The police who directed traffic were Indian Sikhs, with turbans. Many would direct the traffic from booths in the middle of the intersections, where they would manually switch the traffic lights from one direction to another. They were particularly tough on any Chinese who committed a traffic infraction, however slight.

There were many street scenes that come to mind at this time in my life. Street vendors sold fruit preserves, called tucks. The tucks could be sweet, salty, or sour, but all of them were worth trying. The sweet ones were preserved apricots, peaches, plums, mangoes, and other similar fruits. The salty tucks could also be made from plums or peaches, and also from olives or ginger. The sour ones consisted of some of the same fruits preserved with ingredients to make them sour and those made you pucker up. The vendors sold tucks from open containers, and one could purchase them by weight or by quantity. As they would be wrapped in a small bag, or even in newspaper, they would never pass today's health standards. Some vendors sold Chinese candy, which were delicious. Chinese candy was in general not overly sweet, and one could consume a lot of it at one time. One form of confection was a spiral made of soft, sweet date or plum preserve pressed into a flat thin layer with roasted sesame seeds. You would eat it by unrolling the spiral while crunching the sesame seeds and enjoying the combination of the sesame and sweet flavors. That was my favorite candy.

Vendors also sold peeled water chestnuts on a stick. There were about six of these on each stick, and you would take each one off the stick with the teeth and eat it noisily. They were crunchy, with not much flavor but had a pleasant texture, full of water chestnut flavored fluid, which made them a great snack. Vendors also sold salted and delicious roasted dried beans and peas. These were also sold from open containers by weight or by small quantities. I remember eating an enormous quantity of dried roasted beans until I became sick. Another favorite was baked sweet potatoes heated them in a clay oven and hot enough to burn your fingers, but delicious nonetheless. We could warm our hands on sweet potatoes in the winter as we walked to school. We also ate roasted chestnuts, which like the sweet potatoes, were roasted in a clay oven on the street. We would eat this tasty treat wrapped in a cone of newspaper.

But the most memorable of all street vendors was the one who sold fried tofu. This vendor had two stands connected together by a long, strong bamboo pole. On one of the stands stood a stove with a large wok with about three or more inches of hot oil. It was usually peanut oil or some other edible oil and was constantly being heated by a fire in the stove, even while being carried on the vendor's shoulder. The other stand had tofu cut up into pieces of about one inch by two inches by two inches and stacked up in a tray, a container of hot sauce, and another container of straws. The vendor walked down the street yelling *"Chee Dee Ke"* If we wanted to buy any, he put down his load, took some of the tofu from the container, placed it into the hot oil to fry right in front of us. After frying for a few minutes, he took a straw out of its container and the tofu out of the wok, pierced three pieces of tofu with the straw, and tied the ends of the straw. The end result was a delicious crusty snack of tofu. We could add hot sauce to this as we wanted, and ate the tofu from the straw. The whole pack only cost a few cents. That was easily my best experience from a street vendor.

There were many peddlers who sold goods or services. They traveled on the streets with all their products or instruments and loudly proclaimed their wares. Most impressive was the knife sharpener, who had sharpening wheels that were powered by a pedal, and carried on a bamboo pole over his shoulder. When he called, servants appeared loaded with knives that needed sharpening. So he would stop, put down his load, pedal his grinding wheel, and sharpen knives on the spot. Truly he was a pedaller as well as a peddler!

Another street scene that clearly comes to mind is of rickshaw coolies drinking hot tea in the summer. On the corner of Bubbling Well Road and Seymour Road, the municipality provided a large tin container of hot tea with a tap on a stand with a tin cup attached to it by a chain. In summer, rickshaw coolies came by, bare from the waist up, with sweat pouring down their backs, and each would stop at that container and pour himself a cup of hot tea before moving on. And of course there were lots of beggars. Tragic sights, it was impossible to provide for all of them. Young boys reached their hands out and said, "No mamma, no papa, no whisky soda," whether or not they were orphaned. This gives an idea of the British influence on the populace—the British had to have their whisky soda, no matter where they were or what they were doing. It was said that even on safaris in Africa, they would stop in the late afternoon for their whisky and soda.

Chinese children played on the streets, and when it was cold they wore padded clothing. Their pants had a large opening to bare their genital areas, allowing them to relieve themselves when they needed to. I remember seeing many a Chinese mother holding her child over the grating of the storm sewer, with the child's legs held apart, and the mother going "sssssssssssssss." The Chinese trained their offspring well; none of their children ever defecated on the streets, because they were taught to wait until they got home to use the appropriate containers, as their parents did. These containers with human wastes were eventually conveyed to farms where the contents were used as fertilizers.

Shopping in those days was interesting. We didn't go to a supermarket, because there weren't any. We bought our groceries at a provision shop, such as the one on Bubbling Well Road, just east of Seymour Road. My mother called it a Compradore Store. This was a store dimly lit, with lots and lots of shelves and drawers, but not much on display. We had to go into the store with a definite idea of what we needed as was no such thing as self-service. We told the attendant what we wanted, and he would get it. Groceries we purchased there were generally packaged in tins or in boxes or some other form of containers. We bought produce and farm products at a large indoor market with skylight windows on Seymour Road, just north of Bubbling Well Road.

Here we purchased Chinese soups and assorted Chinese dishes. There were food stalls that had Chinese prepared foods some of which were prepared right in front of the customers—"While U Wait"—as we would call it today. But we sent out our cook to obtain fresh fruits and vegetables, and occasionally some of those prepared foods, but only the vegetarian kind, because we only ate kosher meats at home.

We would enjoy many of the Chinese foods available from the market. On occasion, my father would send out to get packets of cooked rice wrapped around a Chinese twist—a strip of deep-fried dough twist, bent into quarters and then wrapped by the rice. The twist was called *Yu Tiao* in mandarin or *Yu Za Kweh* in Shanghai dialect. It was warm and crispy, and tasted so good in the rice. We also got sticky rice, a glutinous rice wrapped in bamboo leaves, which, according to George Wang in his book *Shanghai Boy, Shanghai Girl, Lives in Parallel*, was called *Tsung Tse*. The rice sometimes had a bean paste inside, or would be plain. When it came plain, we would dip the rice in sugar, and eat the rice with sugar stuck to it. It was so tasty! We had to be careful, though, because sometimes the rice had meat in it, and we couldn't have it, because it wasn't kosher. On those occasions, the servants would get a treat. I thought that sometimes, there would be an intentional mistake. But it didn't matter—it was a treat for all of us.

I learned to speak Shanghai-dialect Chinese, from interacting with Chinese vendors and other Chinese on the streets. The Shanghai dialect is very different from Mandarin or Cantonese. Most Chinese learned to speak the dialect unique to their own province as well as Mandarin, considered the principal Chinese language. So I also learned many words of Mandarin. As my amah was from Canton, and spoke to her family in Cantonese, I learned some Cantonese. So I learned to speak in three Chinese dialects, and sometimes became quite confused about the Chinese I was speaking, since each dialect was distinctive. Moreover, I was not fluent in any one of them, although I could communicate fairly well using the Shanghai dialect.

I still remember my good friend, Jackie Levy. He was about my age, and lived on Avenue Road, about three blocks from me. His formal name was Clive Levy, but we called him by his middle name, Jackie. We used to play at his place, or in the lane where I lived, or on the streets in between. We also played with other Jewish kids on the property of the Ohel Rachel Synagogue and the Shanghai Jewish School. We often played with my cousin Albert Levy (no relation to Jackie), and Jackie's cousin Silas Isaacs. At the Jewish School I met Solly Cohen, who was so good at climbing trees and fences we nicknamed him Squirrel. After I left Shanghai, Jackie and I lost contact for a while, but we now share lively telephone contacts. I ran into Solly Cohen at a Jacob family get-together, also attended by other Shanghai people.

When he walked in, I yelled, "Squirrel!" He had forgotten his nickname, and didn't know who I was, and so gave me a strange look when I went up to him. But after telling him who I was and reminding him of his nickname, Solly remembered both me and his nickname.

When I was about nine years old, I had an attack of appendicitis. One day, my right abdominal area started hurting terribly, and got worse the following day. I was rushed to the Country Hospital, to have my appendix removed. I woke up in a large recovery ward with about 20 beds. The recovery lasted several days after surgery, so I was recuperating in this large ward, with my lower right side bandaged up. Any slight movement of my right leg or my right side would cause extreme pain. Other young boys around my age were also recovering from appendectomies, including one young girl. Why she was brought into this ward I'll never know, but there she was. In the mornings, a doctor of one of the young boys would come and examine his patient. The doctor would remove the boy's bed covering and put his hand under the boy's bottom to raise his abdominal area. No one wore underwear. Just bandages covered the incision, and so when the doctor raised the boy's mid-section, his private parts were exposed for the whole ward to see! The doctors were terribly insensitive to the modesty of the patients. The young girl laughed and teased each of us as we were similarly exposed. I was very embarrassed. But one day her doctor came and examined her, and exposed her for everyone to see, too. She never teased us again. They should never have allowed the young girl to be in the boys' ward.

My father taught me to enjoy classical music by playing records on the gramophone. But I am most thankful for his having me take piano lessons. I started at the age of 9. At first I really hated taking lessons because I really wanted to be outside playing. But my father won me over by two incentives: first, he took lessons too, but he didn't practice, and although he could play the piano somewhat, it gave me an incentive to catch up to him. And secondly, he paid me 15 cents an hour to practice! I kept records, and at the end of the week, I would charge him for the hours I practiced. My teacher was Mrs. Fostner, who had come to Shanghai from Austria with her husband and daughter. The Fostners lived three or four blocks away, and so it was convenient to have her teach me, but she endured a lot from me. I would not be at home when she came for my piano lesson, or I would not play or have practiced well, and so had to repeat what she had already taught me. (Sometimes I would hide out at my cousins', the Levys, on Bubbling Well Road when Mrs. Fostner arrived). But she was a fine teacher and, in spite of myself, gave me a good foundation in music. At first it was quite boring learning scales, chords, and finger exercises, even as I had to learn the various symbols on a music page. After a couple of months, though, I actually enjoyed the exercises. I learned to play much of the music I heard on records and over the radio, which gave me a sense of achievement.

My father also instilled in me an appreciation of other art forms. While he didn't do the things a typical father might do with his son, like taking me out on picnics or playing ball with me, he did take me to see opera at my ripe old age of 9. I clearly remember seeing *Faust*. It made a lasting impression. I don't remember much of the opera, but there was one scene in which the devil came to collect Faust's soul after his 20 years' romp of wine, women and song. The scene was quite dramatic; a trap door opened in the middle of the stage, and thick, black smoke poured out of the trap door. When the smoke cleared, there stood the devil, arms folded, in a bright red outfit covering him from his toes to over his head, adorned with two little horns. Only his face showing a black goatee, and his hands, were exposed.

Can you imagine the impression this made on a 9-year-old boy? I can still picture the evil look on the devil's face and that whole scene clearly. We saw the opera in the Lyceum Theater, the venue of many good plays, musicals, and concerts at which artists

from all over the world performed. The Ballet Russe de Monte
Carlo and many other troupes performed there. My father also
took me to see a few Gilbert and Sullivan operas at about the same
time. I saw *The Mikado* and the *HMS Pinafore*. And he would play
some of the Gilbert and Sullivan operas on the gramophone, so I
would be familiar with them when I saw them on stage. For this I
am eternally grateful to him. As a result of the exposure to Gilbert
and Sullivan, I memorized and can still recite a passage from *The
Mikado*:

> *To sit in solemn silence in a dull, dark, dock,*
> *In a pestilential prison with a life long lock,*
> *Awaiting a sensation of a short, sharp, shock,*
> *From a cheap and chippy chopper on a big, black block.*

On occasional Sunday evenings, my father took us out for a
treat. We either went as a family or with my aunt Regina and
uncle John and family to a Japanese restaurant in Hongkew. We
climbed up the stairs of a converted house into a private room
where we were seated on a matted floor. On the low table before
us, the Japanese waitress served us sukiyaki. She wore the
traditional and colorful Japanese kimono and clopped about
noisily in wooden shoes. She cooked the sukiyaki on a stove in
front of us, or on a heated surface on the table. She elegantly laid
out all the ingredients on a large tray, and greased the cooking
surface with chicken fat, which melted on being heated. Then
she placed the meat (usually chicken or fish) and the vegetables
on the cooking surface, in order of the time it took to cook them,
and finally the glass noodles and the sauce. And she also
provided a large container of rice. Adding to the epicurean
delight were side dishes of pickled scallions or radishes, which
were also delicious. What a treat that was!

British society clearly dominated in the International
Settlement along with considerable racism. The Chinese were
particularly discriminated against, but the snobbery didn't end
there. There was even a distinction between British and English,
with English meaning from England, and British meaning from the

colonies. The Cathedral School enrolled only children of "pure European descent." I remember there was always an air of snobbery whenever someone from the Cathedral School was about.

My mother sometimes took me to a park along the river, next to the Garden Bridge that spanned the Soochow Creek. It was a beautiful park, full of greenery. There were performances by a concert band on Sundays. No Chinese were allowed in the park, except those accompanying foreign children. I'm told that a sign read something to the extent, "Foreigners Only" followed by "No Dogs Allowed." My mother took me there once in a while on Sundays. I heard the Light Cavalry Overture by Franz von Zuppe there for the first time. It was impressive!

The center for many sports activities was the Race Course, a large walled-in area in the center of the city. It contained a race track, a large grandstand with a large multi-storied building behind it that housed many clubs and other organizations. The racetrack encircled many fields that accommodated sports activities. There were soccer fields, baseball and softball fields, a clubhouse with lawn bowl courts, tennis courts, and a polo field. All of those fields were within the oval of the racetrack. During the spring, summer and fall, lots of sporting activities took place there. No Chinese were allowed in the Race Course, except as workers or by invitation. In the building behind the grandstand were housed many social clubs. The Shanghai Race Club was there, and so was the Shanghai Bridge Club, where my father played. One could play bridge or some other activity, order dinner, and spend a fine entertaining evening there.

My friends Charlie Stock and Bobby Tchakalian remember seeing a sign at the entrance gate of the Race Course on Bubbling Well Road, that read "Dogs and Chinese not allowed." I'm not sure of the exact wording of the sign, as it appears it might have read, "Dogs prohibited," and then said, "Foreigners Only." Charlie, who had an American father and a Chinese mother, told me that his father could go to the Race Course, but his mother could not! His father had a concession next to a grandstand for softball and baseball games, and he and his brother used to go there to work along with his father. But his mother had never been inside the Race Course. It is interesting that his parents were members of the Country Club, and that they frequently went to the Country Club for dinners or parties or other activities with no problems due his mother's background. The above-mentioned sign prohibiting Chinese from the Race Course has been salvaged and is currently in a museum located on The Bund.

On Sundays, I often went to the Race Course and watched a football or softball game. There was even a football league in which local communities fielded teams. The Portuguese Lusitano Club fielded a strong team there, but other nationalities had teams as well. One time, a top Chinese team called Tung Wah was invited to play. Only then were Chinese allowed in as spectators. I also remember watching the 4th Marines playing baseball, which I thought was too fast a sport compared to softball, to which we were more accustomed.

Another center of activity was the Young Men's Christian Association, YMCA. I went to the Foreign YMCA, as there was also a Chinese YMCA. No Chinese were allowed in the Foreign YMCA, except as employees. The Foreign Y was located on Nanking Road, opposite the Race Course, and next to the majestic Park Hotel and the Grand Theater. It was a multi-story building with a swimming pool, gym, handball or squash courts, billiard room, and a large lounge with a grand piano and tables for card games. There were rooms on the upper floors for transient and longer-term residents. On the street level were bowling alleys and a coffee shop. The Chinese YMCA did not have as many facilities or anywhere near the space or activities that the Foreign Y had. I used to go to the Y during some afternoons during the week and swim or play ping pong or billiards. We were graded on our swimming skills; a beginner was a tadpole. The next level up was a minnow, and then a carp, a herring, a sturgeon and finally a shark. One had to pass specific tests in the water in order to move up to the next level.

There were certain privileges in the pool to be in the higher levels. When the sharks came into the pool, however, everyone else had to leave, as they would swim across the pool and if you were in the way, you would get ducked. I made it to the herring level when I was 9 or 10. The boys usually swam naked, as there were only boys swimming during much of the afternoons. Mixed swimming was permitted on certain hours in the evening and on Saturday mornings and afternoons. At these times, of course, everyone had to wear bathing suits. On occasion, when the boys and even grown men were in the pool, naked as usual, a woman would appear in the balcony that was at a level above the pool. Then all the males would scramble into the water.

The fitness trainer at the Y was Boris Kazamiroff. We called him Girlie Kazamiroff, although I don't know why. He was everywhere, running all kinds of physical activities. Girlie was well known to members of the Y, and is remembered to this day. I met him at a reunion of ex-Shanghai folks in San Francisco, some 45 years after seeing him last, and I recognized him immediately. He had hardly changed! He kept physically active all the intervening time and stayed young.

We interacted with another trainer, Oleg Grebenschikoff, whom we called "Lug" or "Bighead." He coached us on the fine points of swimming—the strokes, breathing and the rhythm—as well as gym activities. Lug was a kind, warm person who had a wonderful disposition, and reflected all his fine qualities when I met him again, also at the reunion in San Francisco. I recognized him immediately as well.

This same YMCA building was used at a later time by the communist authorities as a prison, and possibly even a torture facility[6]. Being a multi-storied and multi-faceted building, it has had many uses in the ensuing years.

While I was enjoying my early years in Shanghai, war clouds were gathering all over the world, especially in the Far East. As a result of the Japanese occupation of the Chinese parts of Shanghai and the Chinese villages surrounding Shanghai, there were occasional incidents in which Japanese encroached on the International Settlement, and the western part of the city would be blocked off. Barricades made of barbed wire with wood supports were placed across the main streets leading in from the west, and in particular across Yu Yuen Road just west of St. George's. This sometimes happened in the afternoon, and so when I got out of school, I couldn't get home. It shouldn't have been a problem as I had many relatives who lived in the area, to whom I could have gone, but I didn't think of them and usually went back to the school grounds and played with whoever was around then. During these times, my parents were frantic because there was no sign of me at any of my relatives' homes and both of them worked downtown, and weren't able to get to where I was. One time, when such an incident occurred and I went back to the school playground, I wasn't there for more than 20 minutes when one of the Cohen boys, whose family lived on Tifeng Road, came to fetch me. I went over to their house, where I was made to feel very important. They fed me, kept me company, called my mother at work to tell her I was safe. It was evening before the barricades were removed and I was able to get home.

Being in an international environment gave me a wide range of experience. In my class in Form 4, there were boys who were American, Armenian (Armenia was part of Russia at that time), British, Danish, East Indian, Italian, Greek, Portuguese, Russian, Scottish, and Swiss, among other nationalities. There were many Sephardic Jews like myself, whose families also originated in Iraq. There were no Chinese in our school. In that year, 1940, World War II had already begun in Europe, but we did not notice or feel its effects until the war in the Pacific and the Far East began. Life went on unchanged. One day, I was invited, along with a Danish classmate named Sven Tarby, to the house of Karanjia, my Indian classmate. In our school, we knew each other by our last names mostly. I was known as Jacob, which quickly became shortened to Jake. I tasted Indian curry for the first time. It was pretty hot but quite enjoyable, although I drank a lot of water. Sven Tarby's family left Shanghai shortly afterward to return to Denmark, I believe, just before the war in the east started. I had a Scottish classmate friend by the name of Jimmy Lootit, whose father worked at the firehouse, on the corner of YuYuen Road and Tifeng

Roads, right next to our school. He spoke in a distinctly Scottish brogue, and was a fine friend. I ate at his place for tiffin, and found the food quite bland. We played in the firehouse now and then, climbing in and out of the fire engines. One day, a German boy joined our class. This was in 1940, when the war in Europe had already begun. His name was Neuberg (or Neuberger, I'm not sure which). In the playground, I talked to him just to get acquainted, and he said with a slight German accent, "Yes I'm German. We are at war. Want to fight?" And then he put up his fists. I thought how stupid that was. I had nothing against this boy, and he didn't even know me! Well of course we didn't fight, as there really was nothing to fight about.

We didn't have gangs in school, but we did play together in certain groups. One would find boys with whom one was friendly and play together, or just be together, laughing or socializing. But going to or from school, one was generally alone. I remember three guys, we'll call them Charles Davis, Ted Johnson and Sam Clovis, (not their real names), who stuck together. They were bigger than most of us in the class, and they would intimidate classmates they would catch alone, going to or from school. They were especially scary to me because they lived and played in an area that was on my way to school, and would chase me, sometimes for blocks. I avoided them like the plague. As they weren't very smart in the classroom, they made up for it by beating up on some of us. One day, however, I was in the playground in school before classes started, playing ball with some of the guys, and Ted came into the playground by himself, which was unusual. Ted was bigger than I was, but that didn't matter to me then. I caught Ted and pushed him against the wall, and we started to fight. I hit him squarely on his nose. I can remember seeing his nose flat against his face and blood gushing out, flowing profusely down his jaw and onto his clothes. When I realized what I had done, I trembled and started to cry, thinking, 'These guys are going to kill me.' But they never bothered me again. All three of them were Americans—my first introduction to Americans—not a great beginning.

We were fairly well off in 1940. My father sent me for horseback-riding lessons, and I was pretty good at it. I attended a school in Hungjao once a week or so to take lessons. My instructor, who was Chinese, gave me good pointers on riding. But the one tip he gave me that stuck with me for years was to control and stabilize yourself on the horse by pressing your knees, not your ankles, into the horse. This tip spared me from many an accident. Because I was so light, my father and the trainer thought I might make a good jockey, and they gave me lessons with that in mind, but I really had no interest in becoming a jockey. One day when I went for my riding lesson, without my knowledge the trainer put me on a horse that wasn't fully broken yet.

The horse was much taller than any I had been on, and I had to be helped onto him. Also, I didn't know that other horses avoided the horse I was on. I rode the horse for a short while, and then we came too close to the horse my trainer was riding. His horse spun around, raised his hind legs and kicked my horse in the mid-section, hitting me on the leg with one of his hoofs. My horse jumped away from the other horse and then started on a gallop, totally out of control. I tried to rein him in but he wouldn't stop. Here I was, hit in the leg by a kick from another horse—for a moment I thought my leg was broken—on a horse I couldn't control, galloping away. But I kept my knees pressed into the horse, and that saved me. Finally, after a short wild run, my horse came to a stop, as I was pulling hard on the reins and yelling at him. The trainer and his horse soon arrived, and I rolled off my horse. Upon examination it was found that I had no broken bones, just a good bruise.

My father owned some racehorses then, and would enter them in the races that took place at the Race Course. At one time he owned four horses: Tattle Tale, Chatterbox, Gossip, and The Sneak. Of the four, Tattle Tale was the best and the fastest. There is a picture of my father and me on page 136 and me bringing in Tattle Tale after he had just won a race. It was 1940 and I was nine years old. My father also had a horse keeper, who would feed, brush and take care of the horses. He was known as the mafoo; *ma* meant horse and *foo*, I believe, meant keeper. My father took me to the races many times in those days, and it always was a thrill to be there. He even allowed me to place a bet for him, but we didn't win anything.

I joined the Cub Scouts at about this age, and then graduated to the Boy Scouts, whose troops were organized according to national origin. There was a British Scout troop and troops from many other countries whose communities existed in Shanghai. There was a Jewish troop—the 5th Troop. I earned two scout patches—one for collecting stamps, and the other for some kind of physical activity, probably swimming. Earning the patches was not automatic; one had to pass certain requirements to be awarded each patch. My older cousin Jackie Goldenberg was active in the scouts, which was an incentive for me to be there. A member of our community, Ezekiel Abraham, was high up in the scouting organization. I remember him at one of our Sunday morning meetings. He attended the meeting in his full uniform regalia. He had so many patches, I don't know how he had room on his uniform or on his patch holder for all of them. I looked upon him like he was a God. The leader of the Jewish Troop was Noel Jacobs; and more on him later.

There were many foreign troops stationed in Shanghai in an effort to protect the International Settlement from threats to its independence. Seaforth Highlanders paraded occasionally in their kilts and beautiful plaid uniforms, and were often seen at the Race Course. They were stationed near there. There always seemed to be a Seaforth Highlander bagpiper's silhouette at the top of the building in the Race Course, playing his bagpipes at the end of the working day. One could hear the wailing bagpipes from a long distance away. The American 4th Marine Regiment arrived in Shanghai in 1927 to protect American property and interests in Shanghai. They often played baseball at the Race Course.

With war threatening, all the British and American troops left by the middle of 1941.Our sole protection now was the Shanghai Volunteer Corps. The SVC was a voluntary military organization that trained, and had uniforms and arms, for the purpose of protecting the Western interests in the International Settlement of Shanghai. It was composed of many units, each of which was composed of members of one nationality. There was the British Company, the American Company, the Jewish Company, the Russian Company, as well as Swiss, Scottish, Filipino, and French companies, and others. My uncle John and his son, Jackie Goldenberg, were members of the SVC. Uncle John was in the Jewish Company, and Jackie was in the Armored Car Company. Noel Jacobs was Captain and the Commander of the Jewish Company.

When there was a threat of incursion by the Japanese surrounding the area, and a blockade was set up, the SVC patrolled the blockaded streets to ensure that the blockades were not breached. I don't know how much protection they would have provided, as they didn't appear to have many heavy weapons or armor, only small arms and rifles. They did have groups called the Field Battery, Light Battery, and an Armored Car Company, but they would have been no match for an invading army. Fortunately, they were never tested on that issue.

CHAPTER 3
WAR

War came to us suddenly and dramatically, early on the morning of December 8th, 1941. We were awakened to loud and powerful explosions, cannon fire, machine gun fire, flashes of light, for about fifteen minutes, and then silence. We had no idea what had happened, and no one called the police to find out, because chances were they didn't know either. When we arose in the morning, there were Japanese soldiers everywhere. They were heavily armed, and had set up a small machine gun and guards at the corner of Seymour Road and Bubbling Well Road. Similar soldiers and armor were in place at other major intersections all over the city. The Japanese army and marines had occupied the International Settlement and the French Concession. They had put up proclamations on the walls of buildings and on poles on the street, declaring the Japanese occupation in 3 languages: Chinese, Japanese and English.

We found out later what had happened. About three hours after the Japanese attacked Pearl Harbor, they swarmed out of Hongkew, the area of Shanghai which they controlled and these armed forces crossed the bridge into the International Settlement. Several naval vessels were in the Whangpoo River belonging to many nations. Britain and United States each had one gunboat.

These vessels were river patrol boats, much smaller than a destroyer, and had one small gun toward the bow of the boat, and not much more armament than that. The American gunboat, the USS *Wake*, was moored toward the downstream side of the other ships, and behind it was a French yacht, the *Gabrielle*. Moored at the next buoy was the British gunboat, the HMS *Peterel*[7].

At about 4:00 in the morning half the American sailors from the *Wake* were ashore, as was the captain, Lieutenant Commander Columbus Smith. A Japanese launch with officers and marines swarmed aboard the USS Wake, giving the Americans very little time to destroy any secret codes or classified material. Thus the USS *Wake* was captured quickly. But the British gunboat was anchored at a buoy some 1200 feet behind the *Wake*, in the middle of the city. The Japanese then boarded the British vessel and demanded its surrender. The British Navy had a tradition of never surrendering a ship, and Captain Polkinghorn was not going to be the first to break that tradition. In response to the Japanese demand, he yelled, "Get off my bloody ship!"

The Japanese captain and the boarding party left and signaled their cruiser, the *Idzumo*, to attack. The *Idzumo* was docked at the curve of the river, with its big guns pointed at the British vessel. The Japanese also had two gunboats and a destroyer, and army batteries on shore. They opened fire again and again, sinking the gunboat and killing about a third of the crew.

The remainder of the crew swam to shore where many were captured by the waiting Japanese. The entire encounter lasted 15 minutes to half an hour. This was our introduction to World War II. It became the second naval battle of the Pacific area after the initial attack on Pearl Harbor.

For the months immediately following the occupation, life went on much "as usual." I still went to school as I did before. However, the Japanese military commander for the Shanghai area issued proclamations indicating that we were under occupation and subject to military rule, and that business was to continue as normal. Shortly afterward, the Japanese began taking control of all British and American businesses. They assigned supervisors to the businesses, controlling all assets and functions. The Japanese, sometimes for military show of force and sometimes by simply stating their wishes, would occupy or evict tenants from apartment buildings owned by their enemy nationals, and even some non-enemy nationals. In the homes of their enemy nationals, the Japanese would enter and then take inventory and tag all the furniture and major belongings, informing the occupants that the property tagged was now owned by the Japanese government.

My friend Tommy Daly, whose father was British and mother was Japanese, lived in an apartment house owned by the British government. They were evicted from their apartment, despite the fact that his mother was Japanese. A Japanese captain and his wife moved into an apartment directly across from us, in the main building, after the former tenant was evicted. The captain often came home drunk and beat his wife. We heard her screams as he threw her around the apartment.

Our lives did change, and significantly. No more commerce was possible between Shanghai and the United States, Australia, Canada and the British Isles. Shanghai, with its preponderance of trade with these countries, had to find other trade outlets. Travel was similarly affected in the following months and years and was limited to connections up and down the coast of China and to Japan.

But the greatest impact for those of us growing up was the source of news, music and movies. We were used to viewing first-rate movies from the United States, although somewhat delayed after their initial release. We saw *Gone With the Wind* and movies with the Marx brothers, Tarzan movies with Johnny Weismuller, swashbuckling movies with Errol Flynn, movies with James Cagney, Mickey Rooney, and Shirley Temple, movies with Deanna Durbin, and Bobby Breen, and lots of cartoons and short features, including those starring Laurel and Hardy and the Three Stooges. Those were gone, and we were subjected to reruns. But most frustrating was that we were obligated to watch Japanese newsreels. The news always began with Wagner's *The Entrance of The Guests* from *Tannhauser*, music signaling the axis' point of view of the war.

The Japanese totally controlled the radio stations and slanted news in such a preposterous manner that it was obviously propaganda. By their accounts, the Japanese had sunk the British navy about three times over, and the American navy about five times. They reported the land war in the Pacific and in South East Asia in the same way. We were used to listening to radio station XMHA, which played popular music and provided us with world news. Caroll Alcott announced the news for many years. He would begin with "Hello, hello, hello, this is Caroll Alcott with the news." Caroll Alcott left for the United States early in 1941, where he broadcast news of the war to American troops in the Pacific. He also went to Australia and there he broadcast the news to American forces. He did return to Shanghai after the war and broadcast news once again.

During the early days of the war, the news was quite ominous. In quick order, the Japanese captured Hong Kong, French Indochina (now Vietnam, Cambodia and Laos), the Dutch East Indies (now Indonesia), Malaya (now Malaysia and Singapore), and were invading Burma (now Myanmar) and threatening India. Soon after the war began, Japanese planes encountered the HMS *Prince of Wales* and the HMS *Repulse*, the pride of the British Far East fleet. The planes bombed and sank both ships in short order, the first time any naval vessel was sunk at sea by aircraft. I was 10 when the Pacific war began, and during the subsequent years, I followed the news along with my father and many other relatives. The news was most discouraging and depressing.

Besides the broadcast band, one could receive short wave stations. However, the Japanese military commander prohibited the use of short wave receivers. By decree, anyone with a short wave set had to take the set down to a designated location where the short wave coils were removed. Anyone caught with a short wave set in working order, could be summarily shot. Fortunately, that military order was not well enforced. Although my family did not have a short wave set, my father knew of friends who used them clandestinely. Thus we kept up with the progress of the war in the Pacific and in Europe.

We also had another, unexpected source of war news. As the Japanese were not at war with Soviet Russia at that time, and despite the protests from their Nazi allies, the Japanese permitted an English-language Russian radio station to be heard. And so we were able to follow the news from a Russian radio station on our own radio sets. This was an exciting time for me. I had a map of the world on the wall of the bedroom, where I used pins to mark the locations of the Allied (at this time only Russian) forces. At first, news was not encouraging, as the German armies rapidly advanced into the Soviet Union. But as the war progressed, the Russians stopped the advance and were regaining the initiative in the war, and also regained territory. This was reported to us in amusing fashion. On XMHA, we heard from German sources that the German armies were making "detaching movements" and "disengaging movements" along the Russian front.

What these were, of course, were withdrawals, plain and simple. When I marked these detaching and disengaging movement points, they were always placed further and further out of Russia and into eastern Europe, and thus closer and closer to Germany. As a result of the Russian broadcasts of this news, I learned the names of their war heroes: Marshalls Zhukov, Timoshenko, Konyev and Rokossovsky.

The Japanese in turn provided exaggerated reports of the war in the Pacific. They claimed they sank the American navy in the Battle of the Coral Sea and in the Solomon Islands, as well as at Midway, and then again in the Philippines. And so it went.

But we experienced changes that more directly affected our lives because of the war. The Japanese set up a puppet Chinese government with its capitol in Nanking. In 1942, this government issued new currency from the bank they established called the Central Reserve Bank of China. We had to exchange our prewar money issued by the Central Bank of China for currency issued by this new bank, called CRB notes for short, at a rate of 1 CRB dollar for 1,000 Yuan. This exchange rate clearly reflected the inflation that had taken place already since early 1941—the rate was about

16 Yuan to the U.S. dollar. CRB notes of high denominations are shown on pages 137-8.

An interesting episode occurred in relation to the Chinese puppet government. Wang Ching-Wei, the head of this government, was considered a traitor by most Chinese. He had a mansion and grounds on Yu Yuen Road, adjacent to the lane at which my uncle Isaiah and Aunt Becky lived. A wall separated the two properties, and my uncle and aunt and family, who lived on the third floor, could look over the wall and see the comings and goings of Wang Ching-Wei and other government officials. One day, cousin Rose was visiting the family, and as she was leaving the apartment, walking down the lane toward the street, she noticed two men standing across the street. They appeared quite innocuous, just standing there.

But when a chauffeur-driven car with Wang Ching-Wei in the back seat drove up slowly, the two men approached the vehicle and fired several shots into the car at Mr. Wang, probably killing him instantly. Cousin Rose, shocked and scared, hid in the bushes. The men quickly disappeared, and the vehicle continued to drive away slowly. Nothing was mentioned in the papers about the incident until some time later, when it was reported that Wang Ching-Wei had gone to Japan for medical treatment. He was never heard of since. It appears cousin Rose had unwittingly witnessed Wang Ching-Wei's assassination!

There was another change in our lives: everyone in Shanghai was in danger of being bombed by Allied planes. The city was so strategically located that we were a prime target for such attacks. At night, searchlights scanned the skies for American planes, whether or not there were any flying about. By 1943, American planes started bombing. At first, planes came at night, but after a few months, they came during the day. The pride of the Japanese air force was their Zero fighter. Zeroes would fly around a lot. But just before American planes arrived the Zeroes were nowhere to be found. Luckily for the residents of Shanghai, military targets such as three airports, dockyards, oil storage facilities, coal storage facilities, and military troop concentrations were located around its perimeter. So when the American planes came and bombed and left, there were pillars of smoke surrounding the city. Sometimes there were huge fires burning for hours afterward. I remember going to the roof of my apartment building and seeing those fires, which were no more than a few short miles from us.

Early in the Pacific War, General James Doolittle staged a daring air raid over Tokyo. The planes were carrier based, and after the raid, they flew over Shanghai on the way to land in Free China. Cousin Rose remembers seeing them and I may have seen them too, not knowing what they were or where they were coming from or going to. One crashed in Pootung, while some of the others landed in Free China.

I prided myself in being able to identify many American planes. The greatest proportion of bombers were B29's. I delighted in seeing them, silvery, in formation, slowly and gracefully flying over us to their targets, mostly in the north, beyond Hongkew. We heard the explosions, and saw the fires and pillars of smoke when the planes left. I could identify B24's, B25's and a few fighters as well. The P38 was a funny-looking plane with a pair of engines, a body in the middle, and a connection from the wings to the tails on both sides. I saw one flying with the formation of B29's. We were later told the P38 was an aerial photography plane that recorded the results of bombing raids. I argued with some of my friends such as Jackie Levy, about whether some of the fighters were P40's, P41's, P42's or P47's. I don't think any of us knew what we were talking about.

The Japanese did put up some resistance as they fielded many anti-aircraft batteries. Little puffs of black smoke, flak, appeared under the planes as they meandered toward their targets. These were exploding antiaircraft shells and produced shrapnel that was sometimes quite destructive and harmful to the residents of the city. A woman in our apartment building was at her sink washing dishes during an air raid when a piece of shrapnel smashed through her window and tore her flesh right up her arm. She had to be rushed to the hospital for stitches. Another anti-aircraft shell used magnesium that produced a white cloud of smoke. It was a beautiful, but deadly sight. I saw one such shell explode in a cloudless sky, creating a beautiful white cloud whose shape followed the shrapnel it produced, reminding me of a huge hand stretching across the sky.

Toward the end of the war, we were subjected to dive bombing raids by P51 Mustang fighters. These fighters were easily identifiable by their clipped wings. I once went to the roof of my building and leaned against the wall surrounding the roof to limit my exposure, and watched the P51's. They were attacking a target in the southern part of the city. One plane dove through the black clouds of antiaircraft smoke, fired its machine guns, and then dropped two little bombs. I saw and heard the explosions they produced. And then another plane would follow, and then another, as puffs of black smoke appeared in the sky as they dove. It was an exciting adventure for me, but my parents had a fit when they found out I went to the roof during the air raid.

Our air raid warning system was somewhat of a joke. A siren that sounded for one long cycle meant an air raid was imminent. Two long wails meant all clear. Seven short blasts meant that an air raid was in progress. At first this system worked pretty well: that one long cycle of the siren gave us a half hour warning before an air raid. But sometimes those sirens misfired: an all clear sounded when an air raid was in progress, or an air raid imminent siren was used to mean an all clear. When we were bombed by B29s, the planes were land based, from Kunming in the interior of China, so the siren warnings were appropriate. But toward the end of the war, we were bombed by carrier-based planes, or planes from air bases set up in the Pacific, like B24's and B25s.

Sometimes we would get an air raid imminent warning, and then nothing would happen, and so we would get an all clear. Shortly afterward the planes would arrive and bomb us and leave, and then we'd get the air raid in progress warning. Long after the planes left, we would get the all clear. One time we had no warning, and planes arrived and bombed the city. As they were leaving, we received the air raid in progress warning. A while after that we got the all clear, but by then a second wave of planes arrived and bombed us. After they left we got the air raid in progress warning. It wasn't until the planes had been gone for a long time that we received the all clear signal. For the entire duration of the war, to my knowledge, the Japanese shot down one American plane, which they displayed in town. But they claimed to have shot down dozens and dozens of planes, although we were never shown any tangible evidence of those. One time, the news announcer on XMHA told us that 20 planes had come to bomb us, 18 were shot down and 2 badly damaged. It was unlikely that one plane was even hit by Japanese fire.

Soon after the Japanese occupation, all subjects of countries at war with Japan were required to wear red armbands, identifying them as "enemy subjects." These red armbands were marked with an A for Americans, a B for British subjects, or a D for Dutch citizens. At first all Iraqi citizens were also required to wear the armbands, because Iraq was a British protectorate. However, as Iraq was not at war with Japan, Iraqi citizens were required to wear pink armbands, indicating that they were "sort of" enemies. My mother likewise had to wear a red armband on her outer clothing identifying her as an enemy subject, and was subjected to many restrictions from the military authorities. Those with red armbands were not allowed in many restaurants or movie theaters, and were prohibited from visiting many other places in the city. But people got around these restrictions by simply taking off the armbands when entering a theater or restaurant, and replacing them after leaving. As I was a minor, I had the freedom to go anywhere I chose. We each had a resident's card, which each of us received from the police station. The card identified the carrier as a resident and had the person's picture on it.

After a year or so of Japanese occupation, all enemy subjects were to be interned in camps. Enemy subjects included American and British citizens, and of course all citizens of the colonies of the British Empire with the exception of Burmese and Indians, as the Japanese were trying to curry favor with Asians to enhance their program of "Asia for the Asiatics." This program, called the "Greater East Asia Co-Prosperity Sphere," which the Japanese planned to implement in Asia, was meant to drive out western colonialists. The program, of course, assumed that Japan would be the leader of this Sphere, at the top of the heap. While the program never caught on because most Asians were suspicious of Japanese intentions, the concept was popular, and "Asia for the Asiatics" was a strong rallying cry after the war. Since my mother was considered British by having been born in India, she and I were supposed to be interned.

The Japanese didn't like to call the camps "Concentration Camps" as that had a very bad connotation by this time, and so called them "Internment Camps." These places were officially called "Civilian Assembly Centers," or CACs. We were issued tags to put on our clothing identifying us as enemy subjects, and were packed and ready to go to a CAC. But as my father was an Iraqi subject, and Iraq was not at war with Japan, he was considered a neutral subject. He appealed to the authorities that the wife and child of a neutral subject were exempt and should stay out of camp. His appeal was accepted. This internment of Allied nationals began in 1943.

During 1943, the course of the war turned in favor of the Allies, which had ramifications for those of us living under Japanese occupation. The Italians, Germans and Japanese had formed the "Axis," which made them allies, but they were "allies" in name only. There was little cooperation militarily between them. The Italians lost heavily to the British in North Africa, as tens of thousands of their soldiers became war prisoners. And Italians showed little heart for the continuation of the war. When the Allies invaded Sicily and then Italy itself, the Italian government changed hands, rejecting Benito Mussolini, their fascist dictator, and replacing him with a government headed by Pietro Badoglio. Mr. Badoglio immediately made peace with the Allies. The German army promptly occupied north and central Italy.

In Shanghai, the Italian liner the S.S. *Conte Verde* was berthed on the river in the middle of the city. When the Italian government signed a peace treaty with the Allies, the Italian sailors on the *Conte*

Verde, rather than give up the ship to the Japanese occupiers in Shanghai, scuttled the ship. This huge liner flipped over on its side, a terrible embarrassment to the Japanese. I remember going to the Bund and seeing this huge white ship lying on its side. This condition lasted for many weeks. Jackie Levy told me that some of the Italian sailors, facing incarceration by the Japanese, had escaped. He had three of them staying at his house for a few days, seeking refuge before moving on to elude the Japanese. They made ice cream and he enjoyed some of it before they left. Jackie also remembers that huge chains were connected to the *Conte Verde* to prevent it from sinking into the mud of the river, and these chains led across the Bund to posts to secure the ship. The ship was later salvaged, refloated by Japanese salvage crews, renamed *Kotobuki Maru* and used by them for war support. Eventually it was sunk by a U.S. air attack near Kyoto in 1944.

By 1944, most British and American citizens were in captivity, in camps. There were camps for families, like Lungwha, where families were herded together in large dormitory-style buildings. These were called "Segregation Camps," to denote that families were segregated as a unit; and there was a little bit of privacy allowed, in that families had curtains around their own areas. But there was a camp in Pootung, (now spelled Pudong), where all men of military age were encamped. This was across the river from the International Settlement of Shanghai. From our understanding, the food was terrible. My father received letters and notes from internees, (sometimes heavily censored) asking for food packages to relieve the monotonous and horrible food they were fed. He responded by sending packages to many of his friends monthly, the maximum permitted. He told me that at one time, he sent 34 packages to various people each month.

Charlie Stock's father, a retired American seaman, was to be interned in the Pootung Camp, but because he was ill he was housed in the hospital of the Ward Road jail. When his mother requested that she be allowed to provide hot food for him, the Japanese authorities granted her request. Charlie and his younger brother Willie would alternately ride to the Ward Road jail every morning before going to school and bring over some hot food, which was handed to the Japanese jailers. Charlie said he never knew if his father received the food, but it was delivered there. On occasion, he would see his father on the terrace, but could not speak to him. If it rained, his mother took the food over in a pedicab. Charlie also told me that his father, who owned a bar and a restaurant, once the war started quickly put the properties in his wife's name. Since she was Chinese, the properties were not confiscated by the Japanese, who would have taken them if they were in the name of an American.

My mother's cousin, Naim Hillel, was an internee in the camp at Pootung. He sometimes managed to get transferred to a hospital for treatment of some ailment, and would send us a note saying he was there. This was a dangerous feat, because if someone was caught malingering, he would be severely beaten. Naim made it to the hospital twice and we received notes from him each time. When he got back to camp, however, he continued to send us a note now and then by means of a paid Chinese courier. The courier would appear at our door with the note which my parents would read, then write a note in reply, pay the courier, and then send him off with their reply.

One Saturday afternoon, with my parents both out, the doorbell rang. I answered it and here was a courier with a note from Naim. He said the usual things: the food was terrible; "they're treating us terribly," and so on. And he ended the note with "How is the war going?" That was enough for me. I was following the war, thanks to my father's access to short wave radio and to the Russian radio station, so I wrote him a long note back, telling him that the Russians were advancing here and advancing there, the Germans were retreating here and there, the Allies were doing well in North Africa, the British were doing well in Burma and India, the Americans were doing well in the Pacific, and so on. I folded the note, tipped the courier, and sent him off.

When my parents came home later that day, I said, "Guess what I did." I handed them the note we received, and I proudly told them about the note I wrote. To my unpleasant surprise, I was verbally hammered by my worried parents because of the many instances of Chinese couriers reporting to the Japanese about this clandestine note-writing. Many people doing this were thrown into jail and beaten by the Japanese. So, for the next few weeks, we did a lot of worrying, but fortunately, nothing came of it.

In any case, there was the ever-present danger of someone being arrested and taken to the dreaded Bridge House. This was a prison that the Japanese operated, widely rumored to include a torture chamber. Supposedly many people who went in did not come out alive. The Japanese authorities would extract information from Chinese captives in order to discover and control underground activity in and around Shanghai, or even to get information about the Chinese underground activities elsewhere.

Another incident took place shortly after my potentially dangerous mistake with the courier. My cousin, Mike Levy, son of my Aunt Sophie and Uncle George, was of military age and also a British Subject, having been born in India. He was initially interned in Pootung, but was then sent with some other internees to the Lungwha Camp outside of Shanghai. One day, he and four other inmates made an escape from the camp. They didn't contact any of us, went instead into the countryside, where they were picked up by the Chinese underground. They crossed much of China to Chungking, where the Nationalist headquarters were, and then into India, over the "hump," the Himalayan Mountains. They were trailed closely by the Japanese, but luckily the Japanese were over one day behind them most of the way and could only go as far as the territory they controlled. All five of them escaped.

Mike made it to India, where he joined the British Army. He parachuted behind the Japanese lines in Malaya, where he led a band of guerillas against the Japanese. He was promoted to Captain at the age of 20, and was commended for his bravery and fighting abilities. But his escape from internment camp caused the Japanese army to constantly watch my family and the Goldenbergs above us for several months afterward. The Japanese posted guards at the entrance to our building 24 hours a day. My father came home from work one day in a pouring rain, and here was this Japanese guard outside, drenched. My father invited him into the building, so he could stand watch in the hallway of the building, instead of out in the downpour. The guard appreciated that very much.

My cousin Jackie, who lived in the apartment above us, was also Mike's cousin and close to Mike in age. Jackie was followed by the Japanese gendarmes for months afterward, in case Mike tried to make contact with him. One night, my cousin Katie was coming home from a date, and the hallway leading to the stairs of our apartment building was dark. A Japanese gendarme stood in a dark corner of the hallway, guarding the apartment. She was quite upset when she discovered him there.

The Japanese enlisted local Chinese residents as assistant police. They were called *Pao Chia*. These *Pao Chia* had certain blocks and neighborhoods to patrol, especially in the evenings. The purpose of the evening patrols was to ensure that there was no light coming from residential windows, as we were required to have blackouts at nights. For us to have lighting at night in our apartment, my parents hung long, thick black curtains that were rolled up during the day and then rolled down at night. Every once in a while there was a sliver of light escaping from the side of the black curtain. The *Pao Chia* came around and yelled at us from the street, and we had to tuck the curtain down properly to prevent light from escaping. We could hear the *Pao Chia* yelling at residents just about every evening, up and down the lanes and at the apartment building.

In spite of inconveniences such as shortages of some commodities, life went on pretty much as usual during the war. We had trouble getting butter, and so we bought margarine. I took an immediate dislike to it, even though I didn't care much for butter either. There were shortages of other goods, especially imported goods. Sugar and flour were rationed. But we could obtain pretty much everything else we wanted from local sources, particularly produce and grocery products. Soon there was an active black market in imported goods, especially those from the United States and England. My father told me that anyone could get Johnny Walker Black Label whisky on the black market for $75 US dollars a bottle. That was in 1944!

During these war years as housing became quite scarce, I learned about the concept of "Key Money." Key money had been around for many years, and it was a means of extracting more money from the renter or buyer of a property. Before the war, if someone wanted to rent or buy a property, he would negotiate for the property, and after agreeing to the rent or price, paid the broker or the owner "key money" equal to one month's rent to gain access to the unit. Rents, however, were controlled, and with inflation they became increasingly less expensive, as the controlled rent decreased in value. But with the shortage of housing during the war, the key money extracted from prospective renters or buyers was now one year's rent, which was due up front. That was where apartment owners made their money.

Schooling became a problem for me. Since all American and British subjects were interned, their respective schools closed. As far as we knew, the only English-language school open in 1944 was the Shanghai Jewish School. There were two French language schools open, St. Jean D'Arc, and St. Francis Xavier; because Vichy France had sided with Germany, they were considered an ally of the Germans, and therefore, the Japanese too. I had a private tutor for part of the year, but I really lost over a year of schooling because of the lack of schools. And then I attended the Shanghai Jewish School, but I had to drop back a year in class for the time I lost. The Japanese allowed the Shanghai Jewish School to operate under their control, in spite of Nazi pressure to the contrary. This was my first taste of coeducational schooling since I was in kindergarten.

At the Shanghai Jewish School, located on the same property as the Ohel Rachel Synagogue, the teachers were quite good. I was in the equivalent of forms 6 and 7, or 6th and 7th grades. We were taught biology, mathematics, English, and there was a course in Jewish religion and religious history, taught by a very serious, religious woman. She took her assignment seriously. She told us of the tragedies that the early Jews faced in the land of Canaan—how Jews were subjugated by invaders such as the Assyrians and

Persians, and described some of the conditions to which Jews were subjected. In one of those lectures, when describing the bleak conditions of the Jews, she cried. I remember the names of only a few of the teachers at the school, but I can still picture many of their faces.

The mathematics teacher, Mr. Radetz, spoke with a strong European accent. He was quite good and got his points across. In those days, however, both my parents worked and were not home very often, and I needed attention badly. Now and then I would disrupt the class. In one of those disruptions, Mr. Radetz sent me down to the headmaster, Mr. Kahahn, whom I will never forget. He was a soft-spoken man with glasses, balding, and spoke English softly and beautifully, and with extremely good articulation. When I was sent down to his office, he caned me: four hard whacks on my bottom, and wouldn't you know it, that day I had worn tight trousers! When I left his office I had difficulty even walking, let alone sitting down. There were welts on my bottom for days. I never told my parents about it.

There were two subjects that stood out in my mind: biology and art. In biology, our teacher, Mr. Valechansky, would dictate to us, and we would write down what he dictated. It was boring. And the next day he would go over what had been dictated, so we were taught the same material twice. This turned out to be a pretty effective method of getting a point across, and thus we would learn some of the biology topics. We learned about petals and sepals and pistils and stamens, all relating to flowers.

The art teacher, Mr. Graudenz, taught us a little about art and art history. He gave us a good perspective on pictures, directing horizontal lines toward a common point on the horizon, while vertical lines always stayed vertical. That was a revelation to me, although now it seems obvious.

We were also required to take a course in Japanese language. Every day Captain Suzuki came to our class to conduct the course. He would start the class by bowing, and of course we had to bow back, and he would say "Ohio gozaimas," which we would repeat. This meant "good day" and was the common salutation upon

meeting someone.   We learned the language, at least
conversationally, quite quickly, and could speak some elementary
sentences in Japanese soon after he started teaching us.

My cousin Emma, daughter of my uncle George and aunt
Sophie Levy, provided me with some of the names of the teachers
we had. There was Miss Hekking, Mr. Holland, Miss Malahovsky
and Miss Moosa. Mrs. Jonah was our homeroom teacher. Mr. Elias
and Mr. Cohen taught Hebrew. But I attended only one or two
Hebrew classes.

During 1943 my mother sent me to prepare for my Bar
Miswah.   My father was extremely unreligious, in fact anti-
religious. He later told me the reason for his negative religious
feelings. There is a prayer that is taken from Abraham's experience
with God, when Abraham says to God that he (Abraham) would
dash his son Isaac's brains against a rock if God so commanded him
to.   The prayer goes something like this, in English: "Blessed art
thou, O Lord our God, king of the universe, for whom I would
dash the brains of my son against a rock if Thou commandeth me."
My father thought, "That could be my brains they're talking
about!"

And he thought: what kind of a religion is this where a father
would dash his son's brains out upon command? How cruel and
barbaric have we become, that we would smash a son's head
against a rock! Since then, however, I have come to realize that the
prayer was to demonstrate one's obedience to God, and not to act
in a barbarous manner. The Jewish religion has been shown to be
far more caring and considerate than that. But it turned my father
against the religion completely, and he wanted me to follow him in
his beliefs. My mother however, was quite religious. She observed
the Sabbath, kept a kosher home, and observed the many aspects
of the Jewish religion and life.

So I went to be tutored by Ezra Reuben, son of Moshe Reuben.
Moshe Reuben was then the Shohet of our community. I once saw
him holding a chicken by its wings and twirling it over his head
three times while saying a prayer before slaughter. The Reubens
lived on Bubbling Well Road, a block or two away from Seymour

Road, toward downtown. I would go there once a week, and Ezra would tutor me on the Jewish religion, and I would learn to read a passage from the Torah. Ezra was very kind and patient with me. There was one drawback in his teaching, though. He was somewhat dogmatic. I was an 11 (or 12) year old boy, very impressionable and curious. I would ask him questions about our beliefs and our customs, and his answers weren't always satisfying to me. Once I asked him why we believed in a certain thing, and his answer was that we were told to believe it that way, and that was that. But he was a good teacher. And I learned to recite from the Torah and understand what I was reciting.

On the Saturday morning closest to my Hebrew birthday, I went to the Ohel Rachel Synagogue, and recited from the Torah. I remember the experience clearly. I did a good job! My uncles, and granduncles were in the synagogue, and after the recitation, I went to each one in descending order of age and received a blessing. There were my two granduncles, brothers of my grandfather, and then in descending order of age once again, there were my many uncles. I think I spent ten minutes going from uncle to uncle to get all the blessings. And then I went home. There was no fanfare, no Bar Miswah party. But I will be eternally grateful to Ezra Reuben for making that experience possible.

A word about the Ohel Rachel Synagogue is in order at this time. It was made possible by an endowment of $10,000 from Sir Jacob Elias Sassoon, and an additional contribution from his brother. The structure was named in memory of Sir Jacob's wife Rachel,[8] and consecrated in January, 1921. The synagogue was on a large piece of property that also had the Shanghai Jewish School and a large playground on it. The property was located on Seymour Road, between Avenue and Sinza Roads. It had a wrought iron fence around it, and the synagogue was located at one end of the property, with the school at the diagonally opposite end. The synagogue faced the back of the property, so that when you came onto the property, you saw the back of the synagogue, and had to walk around to the back to enter the synagogue. The interior had marble pillars and a marble floor, a sanctuary to store the Torahs, and an elevated wooden quadrangle where the Hazzan conducted and said the prayers. There were rows of wooden benches on the main floor. Upstairs there were also wooden benches in several terraced levels where the women prayed. Men and women prayed separately, and only congregated before and after services. A photo of the Ohel Rachel Synagogue is shown on page 136.

My Bar Miswah took place in 1944, during the Japanese occupation of Shanghai. The Japanese allowed us to have a Jewish life, even though their Nazis allies detested us and tried to pressure the Japanese to outlaw Jewish worship and to intern all Jews in a ghetto. However, the Japanese occupation forces resisted the Germans for most of the war.

The Germans sent a Nazi death camp Commandant, a Colonel Meisinger (known to many as "The Butcher of Warsaw"), to Tokyo to insist that the Japanese intern all Jews. He received no satisfaction in Tokyo and so he came to Shanghai to urge the military commander of Shanghai to do something "about all these Jews around here." He suggested that they could be rounded up during the Jewish New Year, when most of the Jews would be in the synagogues and then put into an internment camp. But the Japanese commander demurred.

Finally, after constant pressure from Colonel Meisinger, the Japanese military commander relented and ordered "refugees" from Europe to be interned in an area of Hongkew that became a ghetto. Since 99 percent of the refugees from Europe were Jewish, that meant that those refugees who had fled from the horrors of Nazi persecution, were now persecuted by the Japanese. The only people interned in the ghetto were the European Jews. The two Jewish communities that existed prior to Japanese occupation were not affected: and so the earlier Sephardic and the Ashkenazic Jewish communities of Shanghai continued to exist, unaffected by the Japanese order of internment.

Ghetto life was quite difficult. Jews who had to live within the ghetto had a difficult time earning a living. They were not allowed out of the ghetto unless they had a job or a guarantee of a job on the outside. It turned out that a considerable amount of people did manage to get jobs in the International Settlement. But because of the war, jobs on the outside were dwindling, and commerce, the lifeblood of the city, was quite curtailed. In the Hongkew ghetto disease was rampant, especially dysentery and similar afflictions. The water was of poor quality, and with poor nutrition the residents had a most difficult time resisting many diseases and infections. Upon reading a book about life in the ghetto, I am most thankful that we didn't have to live there. But the residents did the best they could under the most trying conditions. Soon after they settled into the ghetto, small cafes resembling those of Vienna appeared, serving typical Viennese pastries and coffee. The area soon became known as "Little Vienna." A school opened for the children in the area, and shops opened to provide various goods and services, allowing some semblance of normalcy.

The tragedy of the European Jewish refugees confined to the ghetto in Hongkew was that the area was close to many military targets. During one of the air raids, bombers attacked military targets close to Hongkew, and errant bombs landed on residential buildings in Hongkew, killing some of the internees.

As the war progressed, the Japanese became more and more aware of the nature of the war—that the tide was turning against them. But their leaders would goad them into believing that they were superior fighters and would defeat all their enemies. They would receive brave-sounding speeches from their army leaders, or their Prime Minister, Hideki Tojo, telling them of all their wondrous capabilities, that they were superb warriors, far superior to their adversaries. But there was an underlying feeling that all was not going well.

As a result, the Japanese took out their frustrations on the Chinese, to whom they were brutal. There was a bridge crossing over the Soochow Creek which fed into the Whangpoo River called the Garden Bridge. This bridge connected the International Settlement with Hongkew, the former Japanese controlled area, which became the ghetto for the Jewish refugees. The Japanese posted guards at the crest of the bridge, and Chinese had to show identity cards to cross the bridge. They also had to bow to the Japanese guards on the bridge. If for any reason their identity was in question, the Chinese were simply beaten on the spot or arrested. Some of the Chinese, however, managed to even the score in a small way with the Japanese guards. As the Chinese bowed to the guards, they would mutter derogatory remarks about the guards' mothers with a smile. And the guards would then smile and bow in return, not knowing that they had just been insulted.

Life for many of us continued normally, with not much disruption due to the war. We were completely oblivious of the mass deportations of Jews by the Nazis from their countries of origin to the death camps of Poland and elsewhere, the Holocaust then taking place in Europe. Of course we endured the frustrating effects of air raids and experienced some shortages of food products, but I attended school, and followed a normal routine. I'm told by my friend Charlie Stock that the school he attended, the Public Thomas Hanbury School, or PTH, had closed their school building, but continued to operate as a school. (I was not aware that there was any other English-language school open at that time). PTH had an agreement with the Shanghai Jewish School to conduct classes in the Jewish School's classrooms in the afternoons, while the Shanghai Jewish School had classes in the mornings. In the afternoons I would go to the YMCA to swim or play billiards or ping pong in the clubroom.

The summers were great fun. There was lots of activity in the Race Course, in which sports of all kinds were played, in addition to the various activities in the YMCA. One activity I enjoyed was watching volleyball, a sport that the Russians dominated. There was a sizable White Russian community in Shanghai, who had fled Russia after the Russian Revolution. They had come by way of Siberia to Vladivostok and Harbin, and then traveled down the coast to Shanghai to mostly inhabited the French Concession. I can remember watching games played by the White Russians, and was amazed at their great skill in this sport. While watching some of these games, I was introduced to the Russian drink of kvass.

This was a fruit-flavored carbonated drink that had a pleasantly strong fruit flavor. It was delicious, and was a great thirst quencher in the summer. I enjoyed lemon kvass in particular—it was much better than lemonade. In fact, I was so impressed with the drink that I even acquired a recipe for making kvass, long since lost.

Shanghai was a beehive of espionage activity during the war years. While the Japanese had their own agents, and they had Chinese collaborators working for them, there were many Nationalist and Communist agents operating in the city, sometimes in coordination. And although British and American subjects were interned into camps, there were many agents for the British and American intelligence organizations active in the city who sometimes acted at cross purposes with each other. Of course, there were German agents and especially active were Russian agents. The Soviet Union was not at war with Japan at this time, and so was allowed a considerable amount of freedom. For further details about the espionage activities, I refer the reader to the excellent book, *The Secret War In Shanghai*, by Bernard Wasserstein, listed in the Bibliography.

But there was still the knowledge that there was a war on. The Russian radio station talked more and more of the need for a "Second Front" in 1943 and early in 1944. And some of us still had access to news from abroad by way of friends or acquaintances who still had a working short wave radio. There always was some talk of the war wherever people congregated. I can still remember June 6, 1944! Rumors flew around and all the kids I played with knew "something big" was happening, but no one seemed to know exactly what. When by father come home from work that evening, he had a big smile on his face. I can still picture his smile. He simply said: "The Allies have landed!"

That's all he needed to say. That said it all. And then he proceeded to tell my mother and me that the news was that Allied troops had landed in Normandy in France. What this meant for me was that I had many more pins to put on my map on the wall of the bedroom, to mark the progress of the Allied troops. Of course the news from the German sources on our local stations proclaimed that the Germans had devastated the Allied troops, killing and capturing them wholesale. But the Allied troops seemed to have survived all that devastation and progressed through France and Western Europe. I had great pleasure in putting little pins on my map of Western Europe that showed Allied progress.

Our life continued at a fairly normal pace at this time, despite regular air raids, some food shortages, and a great shortage of gasoline. In fact, gasoline was unavailable in 1944 and 1945. So some inventive and industrious people developed the "one-horse power" car, an auto with the motor removed and with tow bars connecting the vehicle to a horse, which would pull the vehicle. And then there were cars that were converted to charcoal burning motors. In the end, the Japanese confiscated almost all the cars to be sent back to Japan to support their war effort. But despite these shortages and some inconveniences, we did not suffer too much from the war. Not everyone was spared the economic hardships of the war. Some of my uncles lost their jobs, and my uncle David supported his family during the war by making peanut butter for sale. We had some of his peanut butter. It was quite tasty.

And then came a shocker. On August 8, 1945, we heard that something called an "atomic bomb" was dropped on Japan. No one knew what that meant. A few days later the same thing happened again. But the ultimate shocker was the announcement by the Japanese Emperor Hirohito that all Japanese troops surrender to Allied forces. Japanese troops were stunned. Most had never heard his voice before. They had been told they were winning the war, that they were superior fighters, that they were driving westerners out of Asia, and suddenly their Emperor, their God, was telling them to lay down their arms and surrender!

First of all, this pronouncement was against the teachings of the Samurai warrior, the code of Bushido, which regarded honor and courage greater than life itself. And secondly, their teachings were that fighting and dying in combat were more honorable than surrendering. Their treatment of Allied war prisoners reflected this attitude: the war prisoners had disgraced themselves by surrendering and so deserved to be treated badly, in the eyes of the Japanese. And now the Japanese themselves were being ordered to surrender. Some Japanese soldiers cried in the streets!

The Japanese military, to their credit, maintained law and order for the two weeks it took for American and Chinese troops to enter Shanghai and take over control of the city. There was no looting of stores or homes, as the streets remained safe. But the Japanese who operated the Bridge House prison managed to slip away back to Japan without being brought to justice. Over the next couple of months Japanese troops were repatriated to Japan, and a new era began in Shanghai.

My father told me an amusing, true story about a Japanese businessman and his family. Before the war, this businessman had some dealings with many British and Americans who lived in Shanghai and with whom he socialized at parties and dinners. During the war, the British and American business associates were encamped in the various internment camps, as they were considered enemy subjects to the Japanese. But this Japanese businessman kept in touch with his friends during the war, sending them letters, and even an occasional food parcel.

He said, "We are at war, but we are still friends." So when the war ended and this Japanese family was due to be repatriated, his British and American friends gave him a farewell party. During the party the Japanese man was asked to give a short speech. He didn't speak English very well, but he could make himself understood. And so he said in his broken English: "I am most honored that you give me this farewell party, and wish to thank all of you. I want to thank you from the bottom of my heart, and from my wife's bottom too."

Chapter Four
POSTWAR

The end of the war brought a new environment to Shanghai. During one of the many conferences that took place among Allied leaders during the course of the war, President Roosevelt had promised the Chinese President, Chiang Kai-Shek, the return of Shanghai to China. And so Shanghai became part of China once again, after decades of international rule, mostly British controlled. The French and Japanese sections, of course, were also returned to China. All of this was to be effected after the war's end.

Shortly after the war ended, my father, who had earlier purchased a bottle of Napoleonic era brandy and saved it to be opened when the war was over, invited many of his friends and family for a gathering for this event. So we had a great party at our place. Many of the people who were interned during the war and who were now out celebrated the end of the war. Our little apartment was totally filled with people. The bottle of Napoleonic brandy was opened and shared by the guests. I was not too young to take part in the festivities, despite the drinking going on.

There were some sobering discoveries made shortly after the war ended. First there were the revelations of the Nazi death camps and the annihilation of the Jewish populations of Europe.

This caused great feelings of grief and guilt among the European Jews recently interned in the ghetto in Hongkew: they survived but their relatives left behind in Europe were murdered. These feelings intensified with each announcement of names of those who had perished in the concentration camps. But another discovery was closer to home. A godown owned by some Germans was found, and stored within it was equipment for gas chambers, and the gas canisters to produce poison gases. No one seems to know for whom the equipment was intended or when it arrived in Shanghai. But since it was stored in a German owned-warehouse, suspicions arose that they were intended for the Jewish populations of Shanghai.

With the war over, I didn't notice much change at first, except the absence of Japanese troops in the city. The currency was still the same, and our mode of travel and daily activities didn't change. What was new was the appearance of some Chinese troops in the city, and soon some American military personnel appeared. I saw my first jeep soon afterward and marveled at the strange shaped vehicle. American army personnel soon were everywhere. And then American naval vessels appeared in the Whangpoo River, up and down the river from Shanghai. Many of the vessels were not armed vessels but support ships like destroyer tenders and supply ships. But the American military presence in Shanghai was soon inescapable.

Military personnel were everywhere. The military command had taken over a mansion on Bubbling Well Road, toward the downtown area from us. The building was used for logistics and support. But I remember the building because in the evenings, they showed movies, *new movies!* So, on some of the evenings, I snuck in and watched the latest movies. I remember seeing *Love Letters* with Joseph Cotten and Jennifer Jones. I slipped into the movies after the lights were turned off so no one would notice me or bother me. Civilians were supposedly only allowed as guests of someone there, and since I didn't know anyone in the military, I wasn't supposed to be there, but I went anyhow, and was never challenged.

In September 1945, I was on the roof of our apartment building, and heard lots of planes. At this time, there were many American planes about, ferrying personnel, materiel, and all sorts of things into Shanghai. But these planes sounded different; they seemed to be coming toward me. And when I looked up toward the east, there were several American fighter planes, hedgehopping over buildings, quite low. One of them came so close to our apartment building—less than 100 feet I would guess—that I could see the pilot. I was ecstatic. I ran along the roof and waved to him, and saw him wave back at me! I am reminded of a similar incident from the movie "*Empire Of The Sun*," when the little boy from the internment camp was on the roof of one of the buildings, and the plane came by, with the boy waving at the plane. I did that too!

I had another unusual experience around October 1945. I was 14 years old, and very naïve and innocent. One afternoon, as I was walking over to the YMCA, a pedicab passed by with an American sailor in it. He told the driver to stop the vehicle, and called out to me. "Hey, sonny." At first I wondered how he knew my name. But I then realized he was using the generic word for a boy. I went over to the pedicab, and the sailor showed me a piece of paper in his hand with an address on it and said, "Tell the driver how to get to this address." I looked at the address, and recognized it to be in the French Concession, off Avenue Joffre, so I told the cab driver in Chinese where it was and how to get there.

But the sailor was a little impatient, and said to me, "Get in, get in. Come with me." Well, I didn't have anything serious to do that day, so I got in, and we arrived at the destination in about 15 minutes. I told the sailor, (we'll call him Harry) how much to pay the driver, and he said, "Come up with me, I won't be long." So we went into this place, and I found myself stepping into a beautiful bordello right out of the 1890's! I didn't know what it was at first. There were bright red brocaded walls, overstuffed sofas, end tables with oil lamps, and the room, in general, had too much furniture. Soon three beautiful young women appeared. They were blond with low-cut blouses and short skirts and looked like they were in their early twenties. Harry selected one, and before they went off upstairs, Harry said to me, "Wait for me, I'll be back soon." Here I was, in a strange place, with someone I met some 20 minutes before, and he had gone upstairs somewhere. So I just sat. I didn't even know why I was waiting there. I said to myself, "What am I doing here?"

A little while later, the madam, a wide, buxom woman with a husky voice, came into the room, and demanded in a strong Russian accent, "Vot are you doing here?" I said, "I'm waiting for my friend." She eyed me suspiciously, and walked out of the room without another word. Then, in what seemed like an eternity, but was only about 40 minutes, Harry came down the stairs, with a sheepish smile on his face, and said, "Let's go get a sundae." So we left and stopped some place and had a sundae. He told me he was from Chicago, and had been in the navy two years, but he hadn't seen any action, as he wasn't on a vessel that went into battle conditions. I knew my parents were going to be home that evening, so I called to find out if it would be all right to bring home a guest, and of course it was, so I invited Harry to our home for dinner. As we were about to enter the apartment, he whispered to me, "Don't tell your parents where we were." We had a nice dinner together, and he went off to his ship. We saw him a few times after that, but by early December he had gone home. He sent a card from Chicago, to which I replied, but then we lost touch with each other.

With the arrival of American military came lots of changes. They brought lots of food, some of which we hadn't ever seen or tasted. We managed to get cans of American cheese. This was a new taste for us. The cheese we were used to was the white, soft, salty cheese that had to be put into warm water before it could be eaten. But this American cheese was edible as it was, and was quite tasty. And of course there were lots of chocolate bars! There were jams and jellies that provided new tastes to us. In fact, jelly was a new experience because we were used to jams that had some of the fruits in them, but these jellies were clear and had no appearance of the fruit that made it in there yet still tasted fruity. Most of all, though, there was the American optimism and exuberance that came with the military personnel. There were easy laughter and ready smiles, and light-heartedness—joie de vivre! These qualities I remember from the days right after the war and after American troops came to Shanghai. I saw an American sailor on Bubbling Well Road pulling a rickshaw, with the rickshaw coolie riding in it, much to the delight of the rickshaw coolie. Spectators like myself and other sailors plied with alcohol watched this spectacle from the street, shaking with laughter.

But there were some more ominous changes taking place. As Shanghai was now part of China, the Chinese were taking control of the city. In the past, the police force had been mostly non-Chinese, composed mostly of Indian Sikhs and western personnel. In those days, the police were quite tough on the Chinese. But now, the police were made up of only Chinese personnel, and there was some resentment toward foreigners. This resentment appeared in the police and among the general population. I felt that resentment directly late in 1945. One day as I was about to return home after playing with some friends, I was on Bubbling Well Road, a little way from Seymour Road when a young Chinese boy about my size accosted me and called me a *"Ngahko Peeseh,"* or foreign beggar. Not wanting to cause an incident, I ignored him and kept walking.

But he followed me, and said in a louder voice *"Ngahko Peeseh."* And I ignored him again. But he persisted, and repeated his name calling, again in a louder voice. And so, provoked, I turned to him and said, *"Noong Ze Tsoongkuo Peeseh."*—*"You are a Chinese beggar."* That enraged him. He had a wooden sword in his hand, about three feet long, and he swung it at me, hitting me on the neck. Luckily, it caused no harm. I turned to him, grabbed him, and slapped him. Immediately, his older brother who was following us pounced on me, and a crowd of Chinese gathered around us. Miraculously, a Chinese policeman appeared who I believe saw the whole incident. And so he said we were all to go the police station. As we were walking slowly on Bubbling Well Road, I heard the policeman say something to the younger boy, something to the effect that, "you know when we get to the police station, he can press charges against you." That stopped both the Chinese boys in their tracks. Their tone and attitude changed instantly. They said something to the policeman, who in turn said to me, in Chinese, "We don't go to the police station." to which I immediately agreed and then went home. Thank goodness for an understanding and sympathetic policeman. This little incident told me that my world had changed and that resentment toward foreigners was widespread. It also alerted me to be careful in my dealings with the Chinese.

By late 1945 or early 1946, the old currency, the Yuan, was reintroduced. During the Japanese occupation, there was considerable inflation, and so the currency, the CRB notes, were somewhat reduced in value. Therefore the CRB notes were exchanged for Yuan at rate of 1000 CRB notes to one Yuan. Inflation took hold almost immediately, and began to run away unchecked, because the government needed money to support its armed forces and thus neglected the needs of the country. Furthermore, corruption was widespread.

Carroll Alcott, the news announcer on XMHA who left for the States before the war started in the Pacific and who broadcast to U.S. troops in the Pacific during the war, returned to Shanghai to resume his position as news announcer at radio station XMHA. His return was awaited with much excitement. He began his first news broadcast, by declaring, "As I was saying when I was so rudely interrupted…"

My parents started thinking about the issue of schooling for me. No new English language schools had opened immediately after the war. The first one to open was the Shanghai American School. So my parents sent me there. It was actually called the Shanghai American Private School then, and was not in the previous campus that had closed when the American school was still operating before and during the early part of the war. This new school held classes across the street from the previous campus, in the Community Church building, on Avenue Petain, or Petain Lu.

I went into the 9th grade then, and as I recall there were some makeshift classrooms in one big room where many classes were held, as well as smaller rooms with individual classes.   Our principal was Mr. Cheney.   He was called Doc Cheney, or as we called him affectionately, Unc Cheney. And he had an adopted son, Jim Cheney, who attended some of the classes with us. Mr. Cheney was a kindly, pleasant man with a sense of humor.

We had classes in English, algebra, modern history, American history, and other subjects. Mrs. Suh taught us modern history. She was quite good in bringing us up to date, and had a student present some topic of current interest once a week. Our American history teacher, whose name I don't remember, taught us about Pearl Harbor, and Pearl Harbor day, which is recognized in the United States as December 7, 1941.   That date is "sealed in concrete in the U.S."   In Shanghai, however, we were across the International Date Line and so we knew it as December 8, 1941, which I mentioned in class. She did not like that one bit, and resented my even bringing it up. She taught us about the War of 1812 between England and the United States, and mentioned that the British navy sailed up Chesapeake Bay, and torched the town on which Washington, D.C. now stands, burning down many government buildings, including the White House. The terrible British! But she never mentioned that American troops went into Canada and attacked and burned many villages, particularly one on which Toronto, Ontario now stands. Of course, this was just the opposite of what I learned in the Western District Public School several years before, when I learned that the Americans attacked many villages and towns in Canada, but that the British attacked Washington was never mentioned. And so it struck me right then that history is written, or rather rewritten, reflecting the prejudices of the particular historian.

The Community Church property was not large enough for us to have any organized sports activities, and so I don't remember any Phys Ed courses then. But the property did have some grassy areas for the students to run around, giving us an opportunity for some physical activity. It was at this school that I met my friends

Mickey Orapello, Molly Lu and Dick Kask (whose last name was Alferieff in those days). We are still in contact with each other after all this time.

It was at this time that I met my friend Dwight Gregg in school. He has since changed his last name to Peretz, the name of his stepfather. Dwight and I became fast friends, and our friendship had a lasting impact on my life. We built an oscillator together, and then a small radio transmitter. That got me interested in electronics. I had learned the Morse code already, and could send and receive messages using the code. While I never became a ham radio operator, I did go on the air a few times and made contact with amateur radio operators around the world, contacting one in Australia, and a couple more in Europe. As a result, electronics became my major interest, which I followed into college, thanks to Dwight and his influence.

In 1946, the school moved across the street to the campus that was the Shanghai American School before the war, and then the Shanghai American Private School became the Shanghai American School (SAS). At first, the dorms weren't quite ready, and neither was the gym. But we held classes in the administration building, which was where the classes were to be held anyway. When I was in the 10th grade, I was pleased to find out that I could select the courses I wanted, a freedom I never had before. And so I selected English, algebra, French, among other courses. Soon afterwards all the buildings were ready for use, and the school functioned as it did before the war.

Of all the courses I took, algebra stands out as the most memorable. It was here that my friends Mickey and Dick and I enjoyed our classes, conducted by Dr. Weiner.

We used to sit in the back of the room and chat, and Dr. Weiner would call us the "Back Row Fools." Algebra came easy to some of us. And so there was little need to study for the course, and we chatted a lot. Every once in a while, when our chatting got too loud, he threw a piece of chalk at us. Dr. Weiner had a slight German accent, and when he tried to explain the concept of a continuous and smooth curve he would pronounce it a "Shmooze" curve, and we all had a good laugh at that. I remember him as a cheery, pleasant man with a good sense of humor.

It was during this time that I was taking piano lessons regularly at home, and became quite proficient. I would have a lesson once a week for an hour after school with Mrs. Fostner. She was a good teacher and I progressed quite rapidly, playing Beethoven Sonatas, Liszt's Hungarian Rhapsodies, and even four hands of symphony transcriptions with her. Mickey Orapello would sometimes come back to my place after school, on the days I had my piano lessons had to sit quietly while I had my lesson—for an hour. He had the patience of Job.

During 1946, many things began to happen in our school and to the communities in general. Firstly, my friend Dick Alferieff left, almost overnight. Suddenly, he was gone. It turned out that his family had an opportunity to go to the States, and they had to leave quickly. Many Americans arrived in Shanghai at that time: business people, military families, and missionary families whose parents went into the interior of China, and whose children were boarded in our school. And so rather quickly our school mushroomed into the school it was meant to be, K through 12. Our faculty had teachers from the States, but also from Britain, China, Germany, and other countries. Our Principal, Mr. Thomas Gibb, a pleasant man who oversaw the expansion of the school to its full capacity, helped implement the many activities that blossomed quickly. In short order, we had music activities such as Glee Club and piano lessons; sports activities such as soccer, basketball, field hockey and track and field, and also drama and dance. This was a credit to Mr. Gibb and to the initiative of the many fine teachers who came to our school. We even had the beginnings of a football team!

I was exposed to American football for the first time on the field behind our administration building. I didn't know the rules, or even the objective of the game. But I knew that sometimes you tackled and sometimes you blocked, although I didn't know when to do either. So when I was on the line, if I saw a leg move I grabbed it. And then I was told I wasn't supposed to tackle anyone when we were on offense. Of course at the time I didn't know what it meant to be on offense or on defense. We didn't have any football equipment then. It was a "scratch game" anyhow, played by whoever was there at the time. One time Myles Walburn was on the other team. He was a giant compared to me, and on one of the plays, we collided and I went down to the ground, with Myles on top of me, sitting on my head! That was the end of the game for me that day.

The year of my 10th grade was a fun year with lots of parties at peoples' homes on weekends, with good food, good music, dancing with the lights down low, and chaperones in another room, if there were chaperones at all. The girls from the States seemed prettier than the girls I was used to seeing in Shanghai. They dressed in brighter colors and seemed friendlier and enjoyed life more than the girls I knew. An air of optimism, laughter and joy prevailed.

When I was in the 10th grade, I met Lily Jacobs. Lily was the youngest daughter of Noel and Dora Jacobs. Noel Jacobs was a manager in the British American Tobacco Company in Shanghai before the war, and as the war approached, he sent his wife and three daughters, Lorna, Freda and Lily, to England and then to the United States, where they stayed until the war ended. He was interned in the Pootung Camp for military-aged men for the duration of the war. When the war ended, his family returned to Shanghai. Lily was lively, with a ready smile and a wonderful disposition. I went to some of the school parties with her, as she was a delight to be with. She was in any conversation in which there was laughter, and often would be the contributor to the laughter herself. She was a superb dancer, and taught me everything I know about dancing: the fox trot, tango, rhumba, and jitterbug. She was great at the jitterbug, and after I learned these steps, we would jitterbug for hours. Sometimes I would go to her house after school, and we would do our homework together. To this day I dance and think of Lily with warmth and thankfulness.

There is an interesting story about Noel Jacobs, Lily's father, which I'm told is true. While he was interned in the camp in

Pootung, one time during an air raid by American planes he stood between two buildings watching planes go by overhead and anti-aircraft shells exploding with their puffs of black smoke. After about 20 minutes, he started to walk back into one of the buildings, and then heard a terrible, crashing, wood-splitting sound behind him. He turned around, and saw that a large piece of shrapnel had torn a part of a building and landed on the very spot on which he had been standing! When he reached down to pick up the shrapnel, he burned his hand!

During this time, the YMCA was still active as a social center, and held dances of its own. We would sometimes attend these "Y" dances, where we would meet people from other schools in the city. I was still a member of "The Y", and swam there periodically. I also played the piano there on Saturday mornings.

Every Saturday morning "The Y" sponsored an hour of co-ed swim time. After our swim, we congregated in the large lobby upstairs at a grand piano. There was dancing; the lobby was large enough to be a ballroom. A few of us could play the piano, so we'd play two at a time. We played boogie woogie, and the dancing went on for hours. One of us played the top (melody), and the other played the bottom (rhythm). Then, someone else would come in on the top, and the one who was playing the top would move down to the bottom and play the rhythm part, and so it would go, with several of us rotating parts—for hours. I don't remember the names of the other piano players, except for Ray Rivero. He was great. He had so many musical ideas, and had such a familiarity with the piano and music in general, that he was head and shoulders above the rest of us.

On Saturday afternoons, we went behind "The Y" to a little Chinese bakery that had a clay oven and would bake Chinese bread—*Da ping*. *Da ping* meant large bread, (literally big bread). It was a round, flat bread with sesame seeds on top, and a thin layer of sugar in the middle. It was about 6 or 7 inches in diameter, and when it was baked, the sesame seeds browned, the sugar melted and together they provided a wonderful flavor. We ate this with a long strip of dough that was deep fried in peanut oil. Called *Yoo*

Za Kweh (or, in mandarin, *Yu Tiao*) it was puffed up and crispy and crunchy. You would fold the *Yoo Za Kweh* in quarters and fold the *Da Ping* over it. What a combination! And what a treat! Some of the adults among us would make a "club sandwich" out of the two ingredients, by having three *Da Pings*, and two *Yoo Za Kwehs* between them. Believe me, that was a tasty mouthful. Upon my return to China much later, I was disappointed to find that they didn't make *Da Pings* any more. They had a smaller baked bread called *Shao Ping*, or small bread, but it didn't have the texture or the taste of *Da Ping*. I was terribly disappointed, as I was looking forward to having *Da Ping* once again.

And so the Saturdays went like that. The mornings were filled with swimming and music and dancing, lunch of *Da Ping* and *Yoo Za Kweh*, and in the afternoons we went across the street to the Race Course where there was invariably some sports activity taking place, a softball or football game, tennis or some other activity.

"The Y" had many clubs which fielded football (soccer) or softball teams. There was an elite group called *"The Y" Indians,* comprised of some great softball players like Charlie Stock, Donald MacGregor, Reinaldo Guttierez, Ronnie MacIntosh, Sammy Tchakalian and many others. They invariably fielded a softball team that performed well in their league. Another club was t *"The Y" Zeroes,* which did well at football. Some of their members were the Nissim brothers, Matty, Shulie and Sammy, Nick Kuznetsoff, and others. I was never much good at those sports, but I was a brief member of the *Zeroes.*

"The Y" also fielded teams in a softball league at the Race Course. The better team was *"The Y"* **Reds***,* which appropriately had bright red uniforms. They were good, and always seemed to do well in the league. The second team, of lesser quality and in the lower level league, was *"The Y" Blues,* which of course wore blue uniforms. I was in *"The Y" Blues,"* never being in the caliber of the top team. I played right field where I couldn't do much harm to the team. Few balls were hit to right field. Once, a fly ball was hit there, and everyone held their breath. Someone yelled "Jake." I caught the ball! It ended well.

School occupied the major portion of my time. It was interesting and fun. Beside the studies, there were lots of extra-curricular activities. We started a school newspaper called the *Shanghai American* or the *Sh'Am*. As I was a sports reporter for the *Sh'Am*, I had to attend many of the games and matches. Club activities included the Photography club, Dance club, the Outings club, Riding club and Dramatics club. We were fortunate in having Mr. Wilkes for dramatics. He was marvelous at directing and coaching those who were interested in acting. And we were also fortunate to have many dedicated and avid budding actors. The Dramatics club performed Anatole France's *The Man Who Married a Dumb Wife* and Oscar Wilde's *The Importance of Being Earnest*. I was the lighting manager for the plays, and I felt the wrath of Mr. Wilkes if I didn't provide the exact lighting he wanted. I worked in a booth above the stage, and one time in the middle of the performance, he climbed up to the booth to chew me out because the lighting wasn't quite right!

Our school fielded a team that played in the American Football League, comprised of teams from the various American military units stationed in Shanghai. The Army fielded the strongest team in the league. The Fleet Weather Central had a team. The U.S. Navy fielded a team either from a ship stationed in port or from a visiting ship. And St. John's University had a team. We were a bunch of high school kids with no one weighing more than about 180 pounds, and we were playing teams of fully grown adults, some of them weighing 220 pounds!

But our coach, Mr. Weekley, whom we all affectionately called "coach," was undaunted. He was a fine coach. Out of eight games that we played that season, we won two, both times beating St. John's University soundly. I played on the team! But I was not much good, and I didn't weigh enough—I was 135 pounds. So I was on the second string, and substituted for the first stringers when they tired. I played end, and I had two claims to fame. First, I completed the only pass for our team in the game against the Fleet Weather Central, a much better team, and secondly, I beat out two Army linemen and foiled a running play by Army. But on the next play the two linemen sandwiched me between them (each of them weighed over 200 pounds), and I was carried off the field. In the latter game, we held Army, the best team in the league, to a scoreless tie! That was our crowning glory.

One late afternoon during the week, around October, as I was riding my bicycle home after school, I rode down Avenue Petain, and then onto Route de Say Zoong. As I was riding, I noticed someone on a bicycle come out of a side street a short distance ahead. He was speeding away and was soon out of sight. I thought nothing of it. It was getting dark. A short time later, a Chinese man on a bicycle rode up along side of me, and grabbed me by the shoulder, and yelled at me, "You ran over the little girl!" I pushed his arm off me and said, "What are you talking about? I did no such thing." He started yelling and screaming at me and pulled my bicycle off the road.

A crowd immediately gathered around us, mostly Chinese, all accusing me of running over a little girl. The crowd became quite boisterous and threatening, and I was a little scared. They called a policeman, and I was to be taken to the local police station. Luckily, a lady came up to me and said, "What is your home telephone number? I'll call your home." I quickly gave it to her, and bless her, whoever she was, she called my home.

I was then taken to the local police station. It was a stark place, poorly lit, and had a couple of chairs and a table and not much more. Three Chinese magistrates were seated at a table on a platform, so they were elevated and looking down at everyone else. I said I had no business being there and demanded that I be released immediately. The first magistrate yelled at me, "Impossible! You have run over a little girl!" Just then the mother of the little girl was brought in, and she was questioned in Chinese about the accident, and was asked to identify me. But she couldn't positively identify me, and soon there was a continuing discussion about what to do. One of the magistrates then asked me where I was coming from and where I was going.

I told him from the American School on Petain Lu, and I was going home to Seemoh Lu, and so it was reasonable for me to be on Say Zoong Lu, and that I was not on the side street where the little girl was hurt. Then the magistrates, policeman and assorted Chinese who were in the room went into a huddle, whispering and mumbling to each other. This conference lasted about a half an hour, and then my Uncle John walked into the police station. What a beautiful sight he was! I have no idea how he found out where the police station was or how he got there. It turned out that the lady who asked for my phone number called, but my parents were not home, so my amah called upstairs and my Uncle John who was home took the message.

When he walked into the station, he quickly took charge. He said to the magistrates in a loud voice, "You have no charge against this boy." Then he waved a small wad of Chinese money at them and said, "Here, this is for you and for her," gesturing to them and the girl's mother. And then he said to me, "Come on, Sonny." And we walked out of the station. That was a scary episode. It illustrated very clearly that power was now in the hands of the Chinese. But it also illustrated the corruptibility of the government officials. And in the eyes of the Chinese population, this was an opportunity to make amends for the many indignities suffered by the Chinese during Western rule. When an incident of this sort occurred, the westerner was automatically guilty, regardless of the circumstances.

Upon leaving the station I remembered that man on the bicycle who had darted out of the side street and sped away on Route Say Zoong. But I will always remember my uncle John, my hero and savior, with great warmth and love. Uncle John was a kind, caring, loving man, and I loved him like my own father.

During those postwar days, Shanghai was a magnet for people looking for work. People flocked into the city from all directions, in greater numbers than the city could support. This meant that a great number of Chinese were on the streets, with no shelter or food. There were beggars everywhere, and many brought with them diseases of various kinds. There was a man on a sidewalk with a hugely inflamed leg, and I was told he had elephantiasis. He couldn't move. Another man, middle aged, carried his mother on his back. She couldn't walk, and so he had to carry her. They were begging too. I would give some of them money, but their numbers were overwhelming. And then there were corpses. Many people who came into Shanghai looking for work and couldn't find it were stranded without food, shelter or medical attention. And so they lived and died on the streets of Shanghai. In the early mornings, a truck would drive down the streets, slowly, and pick up the corpses for burial.

As a result of this influx of people, prostitution was rampant. When women came into the city and couldn't find legitimate work, they turned to prostitution as a means of self-support. I remember that a place at 199 Wei Hai Wei Road was said to be a house of prostitution. And so "199" became synonymous with a house of prostitution.

During this time, inflation was quite high. The government simply printed money in higher and higher denominations to pay their bills, resulting in wild inflation. I had a bill of 250,000 Gold Yuan. And it wasn't worth very much—about 25 cents U.S. A 100,000 Gold Yuan note, worth about 10 cents, is shown on page 139.

During this time most people invested their money in currency that was stable, which was the British pound sterling and the U.S. dollar. Whenever something of value was discussed, it was discussed in terms of U.S. dollars. Because the value of the Chinese currency was so fluid, it couldn't be used as a standard of value any longer. One sunny day I saw a rickshaw with its top up and the tarp pulled and fastened in the front of it. I asked the rickshaw coolie why he had the top up and the tarp fastened. He showed me what was in the rickshaw: It was filled to the top with bundles of money—worthless money—to be taken someplace for recycling. It was worth more as just plain paper than it was worth as money! There were many such stories of bundles of almost worthless money being spent quickly, before it lost more of its value.

In 1948, in order to stem the progress of inflation, the government issued a new currency. The basic unit of the new currency was called the Gold Yuan, implying that the currency was backed by gold, which it was not. Thus when the new currency, the Gold Yuan, appeared, the exchange rate from the old to the new was quite high, 3 million to one. The son of Generalissimo Chiang Kai-Shek, Chiang Ching-Kuo, took over the implementation of the new currency. Under penalty of death, all gold and silver and foreign currencies were required by the Chinese to be surrendered in exchange for the new Gold Yuan. Chiang Ching-Kuo used ruthless methods to enforce the new program, including public executions, sometimes of prominent business people. During the Japanese occupation, there had been considerable inflation, and so that the currency, the CRB notes, were somewhat reduced in value. The new Gold Yuan was originally set at 4 Gold Yuans to 1 U.S. dollar. That lasted about a month, and then inflation rapidly took over.

Many people told me about being paid with great bundles of money that had to be carried in bags or other containers. My cousin Katie Levy was paid with bundles of money the equivalent of $100 U.S. dollars that were so bulky that she needed a pedicab to bring it all home. My friend Charlie Stock's pay was so abundant in local currency that he had a briefcase loaded with the stuff put into the basket over the handlebars of his bicycle to bring it home. My cousin Rahma Levy carried her pay in a suitcase full of this money. And there were many people going to the market with bags of money to do their grocery shopping—sometimes for one day's groceries. Our cook did that. My cousin Leah Jacob remembers going shopping this way. One edition of *Life* magazine in 1948 had on its front cover a picture of a Chinese man at a desk counting money for a small payroll. The picture displayed the man with a small space on his desk to count the money, and stacked on each side of him, about 3 feet high, were bundles of cash covering the remainder of the desk.

My personal experience with inflation can be seen in a menu of one of the Chocolate Shops, an American-owned chain of soda fountains and restaurants (shown on pages 140 and 141). This menu came from the Aristocrat, which was located up Avenue

Petain, a short distance from our school, at which we would gather some days after school. The menu lists prices in Gold Yuan. Menu items are printed, but the prices are typed in. That's because the prices changed every week or sometimes more frequently than that. Notice also that the prices are astronomical in terms of Gold Yuans. Considering that Gold Yuans were introduced in 1947 at the rate of 4 Gold Yuans to the U.S. dollar, this gives an idea of the tremendous inflation we were experiencing at the time.

To provide you with a better appreciation of the rate of inflation, I quote from Stella Dong's book *Shanghai—The Rise and Fall of a Decadent City*: "Sometime in 1948, the conversion rate for an American dollar to a Chinese dollar would have passed the one million mark, and by early 1949 it reached the incredible figure of six million."

A stable source of money was the Chinese silver dollar. In the early 20th century, China mined lots of silver, and then coined silver dollars. Chinese silver dollars were quite plentiful. There were also Mexican silver dollars that found their way into our currency, appropriately enough, called Mexies. We would see silver dollar traders on the streets, jingling a handful of silver dollars. They made a living trading silver dollars. If one sold or bought silver dollars from one of the traders, he would not get a very good rate of exchange. But the rates were good enough that people traded with them anyhow. However, at one point the government made it illegal to trade in silver dollars, and several of the traders were arrested and some were executed, and they immediately disappeared from the streets. But this crackdown lasted only a short while, and after a few weeks silver dollar traders were on the streets again!

The year 1948 started out to be a good year for me. I was enjoying my junior year in high school. Many extracurricular activities kept me in school into the late afternoons, and lots of parties kept me busy on weekends. I would go to the parties with Lily Jacobs, and we would enjoy ourselves with dancing and lots of food. Those were the halcyon days. There seemed to be no worries, just enjoyment. There were fun activities at the Y as well.

I was doing well in school—I received 100 on an algebra midterm—and school was kind of a lark.   And the summer brought more fun in addition to a break from school.

I was 16 and turned 17 during the summer, and the world was my oyster, so it seemed.

But the school year of 1948/1949, brought a change of principal in school. Our principal had been Mr. Thomas Gibb. He was a good principal—fair, down to earth, with a nice sense of humor, and he got along with students as well as faculty, and instituted many of the programs for which SAS was known. Our new principal was Reverend Arthur C. Owens. He appeared to me to be a humorless man, with puritan ideas, and who, it seemed to me, did not have an appreciation of life or living. During our previous school years, a bunch of kids would gather on the lawn behind the administration building to socialize. We would relax on the lawn, some resting their heads on others' laps or legs, or whatever was convenient. We would just enjoy our own company, talk, tell jokes and stories and had a light-hearted time. It was purely innocent, and no harm ever came of it.

Mr. Owens immediately put a stop to that, implying that we were doing evil things, and no good could come of it. That was our introduction to Mr. Owens. I measured people by the amount of smiles they provided, among other things, and I don't remember ever seeing Mr. Owens smile. While I can't remember specific incidents, I do remember that things went downhill from there.

It was during this school year that an occurrence took place that had me seriously worried. Two boys boarding in school wanted to get out and experience the life of the city, and they contacted Igor Lee and me. Igor, who had graduated from SAS a year earlier in 1948, was hired as the Boys' Physical Education Director and was under contract with SAS. I was a senior in high school then. And so we met them one evening, and the four of us went out for a nice Chinese dinner, and went to a place on the French Concession side of the Race Course, I believe it was on Avenue Edouard VII, called the Great World Entertainment, or *Dah Sze Gah* in Chinese. *Dah Sze Gah* had been around for a long time, and had a reputation as a place for good family entertainment. It was still a place for entertainment, but the kind of entertainment had changed somewhat, into mainly entertainment for men!

When we arrived, there were tables with men playing various card or tile games on the main floor. And they were playing rather rowdily, having had too much to drink. We went to one of the upper floors, which offered entertainment of a different kind and spent our time enjoying the pleasures that were offered to us. All went well that evening, and nothing more would have come of it, or would have needed to be said about that evening. Sadly, one of the boys contracted a venereal disease. When he went to the school doctor for treatment, the doctor started asking questions, and reported the case to the school authorities, who immediately started an investigation. When it became apparent that Igor Lee and Ellis Jacob had corrupted two of our schoolboys, there was some serious business that needed attention. We were in trouble.

As Igor Lee was under contract with the school, he was protected from punishment or penalty. The two boys were sent home to their parents in the interior of China. But Ellis Jacob was "right out there," twisting in the wind. I was told that a staff meeting was held about what was to be done with me, and that Mr. Owens was calling for my immediate expulsion from school. I did a lot of worrying for some time. But as it turned out, nothing came of it, and I was allowed to finish my schooling at SAS.

At about this time, our family fortunes took a bad turn. A series of shipments my father had arranged from the United States were confiscated by the Chinese authorities for reasons I am not aware of, and my father lost the total cost of those shipments. In addition to that, some other shipments were received, and my father lost money on the sale of those, too. And so toward the end of 1948, my father went broke. This unfortunate turn of events came at a bad time for me. During my high school years my father gave me an allowance, quite a generous one. I was able to enjoy the things that kids enjoy after school, take out Lily Jacobs now and then, and generally enjoy my teenage years. But this suddenly dried up, and I was hard pressed to maintain that lifestyle. It was especially bad for me as it came at a time that I had a competitor for the attention of Lily Jacobs, and I had no money! I managed to get some money in the form of a much smaller allowance, although I don't remember where it came from. My mother still worked, so it's possible that I received the allowance from her. Work was almost out of the question, as there was little or no work for a teenager in those days. But I do remember that things were tough for us for a while, with my father having no income and in debt. We could no longer maintain our apartment, much less keep our cook and amah.

Luckily for my immediate family, my aunt Regina, her son Jackie, and daughter Katie no longer lived in the apartment above us with my uncle John, and he was lonely with all his family gone: my cousin Jackie had emigrated to Israel shortly after the declaration of the State of Israel. He had left Shanghai in December 1948. Cousin Katie had gone to the States to visit her girlfriend in Santa Rosa, California, and was soon married to her girlfriend's brother-in-law, Dudley Short. My aunt Regina went to work for her cousin Naim Hillel, who had gone to Japan and had opened a business there. And so my uncle John generously invited us to move into his apartment, which was larger than the one we had directly below.

While we were living our lives in quasi-colonial postwar Shanghai, things were stirring politically and militarily. The Chinese Communists had been driven out of most of China and forced to conduct their "Long March," pursued and harassed by the army and planes of the Nationalist's Kuomingtang party of which Chiang Kai-Shek was the leader. For the duration of the war there had been no threat from the communists, as the Nationalists and communists had agreed to join together and fight their common enemy: Japan. But now the communists began to break out of their mountain stronghold of Yenan and advanced into other areas of northern China, receiving support and winning new recruits as they went, to a point that they soon became a threat to the security and authority of the Nationalist government in Nanking.

At first, the communists moved up to Manchuria. The Soviet Union had entered the war against Japan immediately after Nagasaki was bombed, occupying Manchuria and part of Korea. And so when the Chinese communists moved north, the Russians gave them equipment and munitions that were taken from the Japanese during the war. Then these communist armies marched southward, getting stronger as they went along. The China problem became serious enough in 1948, that the United States sent its diplomat and statesman, Secretary of State George C. Marshall of Marshall Plan fame, to negotiate a ceasefire and a truce. Unfortunately, this standoff held for only a short while, and soon the ever-growing communist armies were on the march again.

By this time, the Nationalist government was extremely unpopular, due to corruption, poor monetary policies and financial mismanagement. Many Chinese turned to or accepted the new leaders, the Red Army governance, readily. It became apparent toward the end of 1948 that the communists were a force to contend with, and that the Nationalist government was weak and corrupt. In the field, entire armies of Nationalist troops defected to the communists. One general after another switched sides as the communists approached. Many of the defections were pre-arranged; most of the Nationalists' arms were American made, and all handed over to the communists.

My cousin Joe Jacob (actually my father's cousin, son of my granduncle Saleh and grandaunt Bobbie) was up in the north at this time. He was a correspondent for the United Press, and able to speak to the communist troops in Chinese. However, he was discovered sending reports back to the States that the communists considered unfavorable to them, and was subsequently blacklisted and denied access. By the time the communists reached the Yangtze River, Joe was the United Press Bureau Chief in Nanking, in December 1948. He was warned to get out; the communists had put a price on his head. So he immediately left Nanking, came to Shanghai, married his fiancée and got on the first boat taking emigrants to Israel, the *Wooster Victory*.

Early in 1949, the State Department of the United States issued warnings to Americans with non-essential responsibilities to leave China, and many heeded the warning. Other western nations followed with similar warnings to their citizens. Many of those subjects left. There were dire warnings of troubles, incarceration, torture and even killings, and so the populace of westerners started an exodus early in 1949.

Chapter Five
Life Under Communism

Early in 1949, the situation looked bleak for the western population of Shanghai. With daily reports of communist armies advancing from the north and headed mostly toward Nanking and Shanghai, citizens of western nations began to think about their future and safety in a new and changing environment, and the attitudes of most foreigners became dour and depressed. An exodus began, with daily reports of people leaving for other parts of the world, by boat, by plane or by train.

This exodus had a devastating effect at SAS. The American Consulate had issued a warning to American citizens early in 1949 that the situation was fluid and changing rapidly, and that it might be unsafe for non-essential personnel to remain in Shanghai. I believe that the British Consulate issued a similar warning to its citizens. Thus my American classmates began leaving, and our class sizes quickly diminished, sometimes down to just three or four. The most depressing time for me was when Lily Jacobs left with her family for Japan. Although I don't remember their departure date, I do remember that it was a weekday, when I was in school. I missed her smiling face, her lively personality, and especially her uplifting disposition. Our school pressed on as well as we could. Classes were held as though nothing was happening, although class sizes were being decimated. And then some teachers left, and some classes had to be cancelled.

The military and political situation became increasingly dire by March 1949, and was degenerating rapidly as the communist armies continued to sweep southward toward Nanking and Shanghai. The Nationalist military commander for the Shanghai area issued strong pronouncements that the city would be defended and that no one needed to worry about their safety. Nevertheless, there was a general feeling of unease that permeated all activities,and conversations.

Finally, by late April and into early May, communist armies, which had been inexorably approaching Shanghai and growing in strength, entered the villages surrounding Shanghai. The "unthinkable" was happening! While communism had taken hold in Russia, and after the war expanded into Eastern Europe, few really expected communists to take over a large and religiously oriented country like China, and certainly not such a cosmopolitan and economically vibrant city as Shanghai. In Shanghai, capitalism had always ruled, and western influences had dominated city life for over a century. Shanghai, the Pearl of the Orient! The Paris of the east! The only city in China with its own Chinatown! Western architecture was pervasive in Shanghai, although there were some Chinese touches to it. Every major building had a western motif and was designed by a western architect. The International Settlement and the French Concession were really western cities carved out of China. But it was happening. Shanghai was being slowly cut off from the rest of the world. It was as if a noose was tightening around the city.

On the eve of the communists' final thrust to take over the city, the Nationalists prepared for a quiet evacuation of Shanghai. While they were heavily focusing on defending the downtown area until they managed to leave with the wealth of the city and of the country, the Nationalists had brought in some ships into which they loaded gold bullion during the night. When the ships were fully loaded and Nationalist bigwigs safely on board, the ships left for Taiwan, leaving behind a rear guard to slow the takeover of the city.

At last, the takeover began. I heard explosions, many of them, that seemed to come from the west and the south. There were also small arms fire, machine guns, and rifles. It happened overnight; at least, it seemed that way. The firing moved across the city as the communists slowly dislodged the little Nationalist resistance, until an eerie silence ensued. The communist troops marched into the city from the French Concession on May 25, 1949. I noted soldiers, dressed in faded green uniforms, with caps that had a red star. They were everywhere, looked sullen and unfriendly, armed with rifles, but generally did not interfere with street activity. They appeared extremely well disciplined. Life went on as usual, at least for a while. No one knew what would happen next, and everyone seemed to regard the change with apprehension.

At first, conditions actually improved. Suddenly, there were no beggars on the streets, because they had been rounded up and given food and medical attention. The vast amounts of prostitutes were taken to centers at which they were told that their profession was not an honorable way to earn a living. The prostitutes were then given food and medical attention and "honorable" work. The communist army had a huge number of men under arms, rumored to be over a million at the time. These men needed uniforms, so the former prostitutes sewed them. Prices stabilized. At first a black market for many goods emerged, but the authorities effectively and quickly eliminated the practice.

The Communists introduced a new currency, called *Jen Min Piao*, or People's Bank Money, and we called it JMP notes. (It has since been changed to the mandarin dialect and called *Ren Min Bi*, or RMB, and was revalued circa 1953). When the JMP notes were first introduced, the exchange rate of Gold Yuan to JMP was 100,000 Gold Yuans to 1 JMP! This rate reflects the inflation rampant in the final days of Nationalist control.

Overnight, the attitude of the Chinese population changed drastically. A decidedly strong anti-foreign tone entered into dealings between Chinese and westerners. Westerners were regarded as the foreign devils who had dominated China and the Chinese for too long. Western influence was regarded as evil.

Shopping, which had been a necessary and somewhat pleasant activity in the past, became an unpleasant and often a frustrating experience. Chinese shopkeepers would serve Chinese first, and only after all Chinese patrons had been served were Westerners attended to. Chinese employees of many businesses took over the businesses, often locking their former supervisors in their offices and not allowing them out until the employees extracted concessions from them. Going to work soon became a harrowing experience. The Chinese employees often had the sympathy and support of the new police or local authorities, so whenever a dispute occurred, the foreigner was always wrong, regardless of the situation.

Slowly, Communist control of the city took shape. Managers of businesses, whether Chinese or foreign, were told by the authorities to cooperate with them, and that if they didn't, they would be dealt with harshly. This was especially true of Chinese managers, because they were formerly supportive of the Nationalists, and had to be indoctrinated into communist thinking. I read one report years later indicating that Shanghai's Communist leaders told the many Chinese businessmen and managers of factories and workshops that if they didn't cooperate with the authorities they would be eliminated. Cooperation became imperative for survival.

Another effective method of gaining control of the city was through the strict imposition of property taxes. Under Nationalist control, the authorities had been quite lax in imposing and collecting taxes because those authorities were corrupt and could be bribed and bought off in many ways. However, the Communist leaders called in the owners of various properties and told the owners, "Our records indicate that you haven't paid taxes on your property for the last ten years, and you owe back taxes in the amount of …" Conveniently for the Communist authorities, the amount of back taxes exceeded the values of the properties, and so the authorities easily took over control and ownership of private property.

Since Communist takeover of the city occurred early on May 25, 1949, my school year was still in progress. Luckily, a decision was made to continue and complete the academic year. On Saturday, May 28, 1949, graduation took place in the auditorium of the Shanghai American School. Eleven students marched down the aisle to receive their graduation diplomas, myself included— about half of the original class. I treasure that diploma.

But the future looked increasingly bleak for foreigners in Shanghai. The Communist authorities closed the port of Shanghai. This was probably done in response to the Nationalist blockade of the mouth of the Yangtze River. For a city whose entire being is based on commerce, shipping, trade, import/export, to close the port of Shanghai is to kill the economical life of the city. Shanghai, whose normal productive output dwarfed that of Hong Kong, Tokyo, Singapore, or *all three cities combined*, fell into a depressed state as a result of the closure of the port of Shanghai and the mining of the mouth of the Yangtze River by the Nationalists. And so, upon graduation, I had thoughts of going elsewhere for my future. The only university available to me in Shanghai was St. John's University, and this did not provide an appealing option, because it meant remaining in an area where I would not be welcome, and possibly persecuted. There was also the possibility, even the probability, that the university would be closed by the Communist authorities.

I still had the summer before me, and I chose to enjoy it and put off making any serious decisions regarding my future. Summer was always pleasant in Shanghai. There was the YMCA and the Race Course, along with their associated activities. But this time it was different. There were far fewer people who attended the Y and the Race Course. So many of my friends had left and so few remained that an emptiness now permeated my world.

Shanghai became the pearl of the communist world. It was reported that the Chinese ambassador to Soviet Russia was congratulated, feted, wined and dined, and even bounced up and down on a blanket after the occupation of Shanghai. Shanghai was and is the largest, most populated city under Communist control. In July 1949, the People's Liberation Army staged a victory parade down the main street of Shanghai, Nanking Road, and its continuation, Bubbling Well Road. The parade lasted about seven hours, and was rumored to have 100,000 troops marching in it, an impressive military display. At the head of the parade was the Commander of the PLA, General Chu Teh. There were no tanks or heavy armor, just foot soldiers, thousands upon thousands of them, both on foot and conveyed in trucks. The soldiers in trucks sometimes sang rousing communist slogans.

After the victory parade, the authorities got down to consolidating their position in Shanghai, further extending their authority over the population. I felt a distinctly negative attitude in many dealings I had with Chinese. The street vendors or shopkeepers seemed to regard me and other foreigners with disdain, even contempt. We were the "foreign devils" after all.

Not surprisingly, it soon became apparent that we might have to leave China. My father was having a difficult time earning a living, and there appeared no end in sight to an increasingly dismal outlook for the future. So my mother and I applied for exit visas— we had to do that in order to have permission to leave. My father planned to stay in the hope that the new regime would see the need for trade and reopen the port. We lived in a formerly strongly British-influenced society, and the British were traders by nature, perennially optimistic about trading with the world. That's probably because the British Isles needed to trade with the world in order to obtain the necessities for their society, and thus developed good trading customs and procedures. My father's attitude was that the Communists would soon open the port of Shanghai, and "we'll trade with them." Many westerners who chose to stay had that same attitude.

The problem was that my father was broke, and we couldn't afford the passage for my mother and myself to leave for an overseas location. I hoped my uncles Aaron and Moses Jacob would provide for our passage, if and when the time came for that. Another problem was that it took many months to have an exit visa issued, and no one knew when or if a ship would be allowed to come in to take those who wished to leave. My mother and I applied for an exit visa anyhow.

There were so many uncertainties in those days, and even though I was only 17 at the time, I felt a great degree of insecurity. Where would we go? How would we live? Where would the money come from? I had no outstanding skills, having just graduated from high school, although my mother was a very proficient stenographer. Which country would take us? I had applied for emigration to the United States in 1947, but I had no illusions about when my immigration quota number would come up. With the current turn of events, how was the United States going to respond to applicants from a Communist-held China? In those days, the United States had a quota system based on country of birth. There were so many people of western origin born in China that the U.S. established a special quota for them, called the White Chinese quota. (It was formally called the Non-Racial quota).

The White Chinese quota was set at 105 individuals per year. But hundreds of people applied. The quota system was such that an applicant was assigned a number dependent upon when the person applied to emigrate to the U.S.—the earlier he or she applied, the lower the number, and the sooner he/she was allowed to enter the U.S. I had no idea where in the line I was, but I was told that the average waiting time for emigration to the U.S. for White Chinese was 5 years! I had applied in 1947, so I could expect to enter the U.S. in 1952, on the average –3 years into the future. Further complicating the quota was that priority was given to GI brides, so that those of us not in that category would be pushed back in the sequence, and each year's quota was rapidly used up.

Another uncertainty was my passport. In 1947, when I had applied for an immigration number, I had to have a valid passport. In those days, we were under a Chinese Nationalist government, which was not highly regarded. I had an opportunity to choose between having Chinese or Iraqi citizenship, and so with my father's recommendation, I chose Iraqi citizenship and obtained an Iraqi passport. In 1948, with the proclamation of the State of Israel, Iraq was rabidly anti-Israel, declaring that no Iraqi passports would be renewed for Jews, and that one had to go to Iraq to renew one's passport. My Iraqi passport was due to expire on April 25, 1950, having been renewed twice by the British Consul-General in Shanghai. There was no way I was going to Iraq to renew my passport.

No one knew exactly when his or her quota number would come up, or how long it would take. The 5-year wait was not a certainty. It was an approximation at best.

I passed the summer of 1949, trying to make the best of it, all the time carrying this weight of uncertainty. The summer went slowly. A typhoon with very strong winds dropped a vast amount of rain on the city, flooding many streets. The storm put a damper on everyone and everything. Once it was over, I spent a lot of time taking care of the various approvals, visas, certificates of vaccinations and inoculations, and sundry bureaucratic requirements. I had the good fortune to get a visitor's visa to Canada, good for six months, which had to be presented to Canadian authorities within four months from the issuing date. I also acquired a visa to pass through the United States on the way to Canada; vaccinations against smallpox, typhoid and cholera. I finally received my exit visa from the communist authorities on September 19, 1949. It was valid until October 18, 1949.

During the summer, persistent rumors surfaced that the American President Lines (APL) was granted permission to bring in a ship to carry those who wanted to leave. Late in September the APL ship, the *General Gordon* arrived in Shanghai, to transport out those westerners who had exit visas. We were going to be allowed to board and leave Shanghai after all! The vessel was a converted troopship and was brought in to take out State Department and consular personnel. There was a large amount of additional space, and could accommodate those who could leave, and who had legitimate entry into the United States including a group of Jewish "refugees" who would be allowed to travel across the United States "In Bond." This meant that they would not set foot on American soil—literally, and physically—and would traverse the U.S. on a sealed train, unable to alight from the train until it reached its destination, in this case in Canada. My grandaunt Bobbie and cousin Rose Jacob, and my aunt Sophie and cousins Katie, Emma and Albert, all Levys, would take that train.

It appeared my parents had solved the problem of our passage fares. I'm not sure who paid for our passages, but my mother and I had our fares paid for, probably by one or more of my uncles on the Jacob side. We began to pack and had to decide what we were going to take. The Chinese authorities allowed no evidence or information detrimental to China to leave the country. They scrutinized photographs, scrapbooks, albums and the like, sometimes disallowing certain articles or photos to be taken out. So we packed with an eye for such a restrictions. My mother had packed hand-embroidered tablecloths, two silver tea sets, one with a dragon motif and another with a bamboo design, Chinese vases and many such articles of Chinese origin. None of them was very valuable, and there were no antiques.

I had an album with photographs of many sites in Shanghai, yearbooks from high school. We didn't know which, if any, of these items would be disallowed or even confiscated by the authorities, so we packed them to make it most inconvenient to unpack and check. We took one big trunk and a few suitcases. My mother and I had $100 in U.S. currency between us. We weren't even sure if we would be allowed to take that out of the country.

People planning to leave China had to post a notice of intent in the local newspapers. Creditors could then report their monetary claims against a person, which then needed to be satisfied My mother and I did this in separate advertisements.

The day finally arrived when we were to leave. The *General Gordon* had arrived, docked on a pier on the Whangpoo. My parents and I went down to the dock with our luggage: a large trunk and separate suitcases. The *General Gordon* towered over everyone, with separate gangplanks for passengers and luggage to board the ship. Tables had been set up by the authorities in a customs shed, manned by men in uniform with lists of people approved for departure. Hundreds of people lined up to be cleared by the authorities and checked out for possession of the appropriate permits and visas.

My mother cleared easily. Her passport, visas and immunization records were in order. When I was checked, a shocker happened; someone had made a financial claim against me! I was stunned. I had no debt; I was 18 years old, without financial activity of any consequence in my life. However, at least 3 other Ellis Jacobs lived in Shanghai—my uncle, myself, other Ellis Jacobs from two other Jacob families living on Seymour Road, and possibly another one from the Jacob family from Persia. Apparently one of the others had a debt or financial obligation of some sort, but not me! Someone made a claim against Ellis Jacob. The authorities were not going to let me go. They did not indicate the nature or the amount of the financial claim, only that there was a claim against me. My mother was ready to board the ship, but I couldn't go! This was too much.

Added to the emotional stress of departure from the only city I ever knew, without my father going with us, heading to an unknown future in an unknown location, I wasn't even allowed to leave! Thus held up, I just started to cry, openly and loudly. My father saved the day. He told the agent with the list of names that he would guarantee payment of any claim made against me, and he was willing to sign a statement to that effect. He provided his name and address, identifying himself as my father and guarantor. That seemed to satisfy the man with the list, he allowed me to board. Thus ended a harrowing experience!

We were forbidden to take any Chinese currency out of the country—even though it was worth almost nothing in terms of U.S. dollars: the exchange rate of JMP to the US dollar at that time was about 23,000 JMP to 1 US dollar. So my mother and I gave my father whatever local currency we had, which wasn't much.

We were with runaway inflation, not only during the period of communist rule, but during the 8 years with 4 different governments. I managed to obtain a 1-cent piece. It is a piece of paper, 1" x 3," red, issued by the Central Bank of China around 1940. This is illustrated on page 142. I remember that one could buy things with it—not much, but something. For instance, it bought a piece of candy, a dumpling, some tucks, or some trinkets. One time I calculated the value, (or the devaluation) of that one-cent piece over some eight years, at the official exchange rates over the four currencies we had. I found that that 1-cent piece was worth 1/100-trillionth of a U.S. dollar at the time that we left Shanghai! The Yuan at the time the 1-cent piece was issued was worth one sixteenth of a U.S. dollar. Does this example give you an idea of the wild inflation we experienced over those eight years? Pages 143-145 show a 5 cent piece and 5 and 10 Yuan notes, respectively

Aboard the *General Gordon,* the American government personnel were given first class accommodations, while the rest of the passengers were placed typical troop-style facilities. Men and women were separated in the holds. There were large areas with bunks suspended from the ceilings, three high. I was fortunate; I had the middle bunk. Thus I didn't have to climb to the top bunk, or have someone stepping on the lowest bunk during bedtime. I remember that each person had a pillow and a blanket, and that was sufficient because the hold was warmed and quite comfortable. The area included a communal bathroom, with multiple toilets and many basins, although there was not much privacy.

I immediately went up to the deck to wave goodbye to my father, and meet other passengers I knew. My cousins the Levy's and their mother, my aunt Sophie, were on board, and I met Albert on deck. My mother was also on the deck, waving to my father. Soon the deck was crowded with people jostling each other and jockeying for position at the railing to see those on the dock and to wave goodbye one last time.

Much of the Jacob clan emigrated: my uncle Moses and his wife Rachel were on board, and my uncle Solomon, his wife Helen, Uncle Aaron and his wife Rachel, cousin Rose and her mother, Auntie Bobbie. Even distant cousins, the Ezekiels, were leaving. Raymond Ezekiel was my age and a good friend. His older brother, Noel Ezekiel, whom I knew only slightly, was there. He was to be a good friend of mine in the future. There were others whom I knew, some from SAS. Our principal from SAS, Mr. Owens, was aboard, as were some of the former students from classes behind me. In all, there were literally hundreds of people leaving Shanghai on that boat. On September 25th or 26th (I'm not sure which) the *General Gordon* left Shanghai, and I was on my way to a new life in the Western Hemisphere.

The trip across the Pacific Ocean took about 3 weeks. We landed in Hong Kong, then Tokyo and Honolulu, and finally, San Francisco. It was an exciting time. When we landed in Hong Kong, I went ashore with Raymond Ezekiel and his brother Noel. We spent the day wandering about the city and visited the Tiger Balm Gardens, atop a mountain. We had to travel up by cable car, and the view was spectacular. When we arrived in Tokyo, we were met by hundreds of people at the dock, among them Lily Jacobs. I was taken to her home, where I was fed lunch and spent a nice afternoon at her home with her and her family.

In Honolulu I went with my mother and uncle Moses and aunt Rachel and the Ezekiels to a beach associated with a hotel on Waikiki Beach, with a fantastic view of Diamond Head.

The day before we arrived in San Francisco, we were hit by a strong gale, and the ship rolled from side to side. I became really seasick and couldn't hold down any food that day. I was pretty miserable. But going under the Golden Gate Bridge was a tonic for everyone, regardless of how seasick anyone was the day before. Landing in San Francisco meant the end of my Shanghailander status and the beginning of a brand new status for me. But in a sense I will always be a Shanghailander—it was my home town, and it was part of me, with all its faults and merits.

Consular fee stamps to the value of the fees charged must be affixed to this form and cancelled.

British Consul's District of H.B.M. Consulate General, Shanghai.

Marriage solemnized at H.B.M. Consulate General.

No.	When Married.	Name and Surname.	Age.	Condition.	Rank or Profession.	Residence at the time of Marriage.	Father's Name and Surname.	Rank or Profession of Father.
32	April 7, 1903	Jacob Isaack Jacob	33	Bachelor	Mercantile Clerk	Shanghai	Isaack Jacob	(deceased)
		Aziza Sassoon Ezekiel Abraham	15	Spinster	—	Shanghai	Sassoon Ezekiel Abraham	Priest

Married in the Consulate General according to the Rites and Ceremonies of the Foreign Marriage Oct 1892, by me,

Provisions

This Marriage was solemnized between us,

(sd) J. J. Jacob
(sd) Aziza S.E. Abraham

In the Presence of us,

(sd) D. E. J. Abraham
(sd) S. I. Solomon

(sd) J. W. Jamieson
Acting Consul General

I, J. W. Jamieson, , His Britannic Majesty's Consul, Acting Consul General at Shanghai, do hereby certify, That this is a True Copy of the Entry of the Marriage of Jacob Isaick Jacob and Aziza Sassoon Ezekiel Abraham, Number 32, in the Register Book of Marriages kept at this Consulate.

Witness my Hand and Seal this seventh day of April, 1903.

The marriage certificate of my Jacob grandparents. Note that it was administered and signed by the British Consul General.

My aunt Regina on the left and
my mother, taken in the 1920s

My Levy grandfather, Abooyee.

My uncle George Levy, and aunt Sophie

My parents' wedding picture. My uncle John and aunt Regina are on the extreme left, and their children, Jackie and Katie are at the front left.

The Bund. The most famous street in China. Photo courtesy of SinoMedia Shanghai

Myself at about 3 years old.

My 7th birthday party.
I am on a chair in the center, with a paper hat on my head.
My friend, Jackie Levy is seated with his arms folded, on the right.

The Jacob clan atop the roof of the apartment building on Rue Dufour. I
am the little boy sitting on my mother's lap.

The Ohel Rachel Synagogue, as seen upon entering the property. Entry to the Synagogue is around to the rear. I was Bar Miswah-ed in the Synagogue in 1944, under Japanese occupation

I was 9 years old when my father and I led Tattle Tale in as the winner of the race. The mafoo is at the left.

5000 Yuan CRB note, printed by the Japanese puppet government of
China during World War II, used in Japanese occupied territory

10,000 Yuan CRB note

100,000 Gold Yuan note, printed by the Nationalist government of
Chiang Kai-Shek, eventually worth about 10 cents

 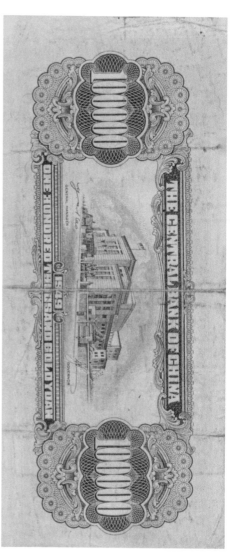

ARISTOCRAT CHOCOLATE SHOP

FROM OUR KITCHEN

WAFFLES	Special 3 LAYER TOASTED Sandwiches
SERVED	Chicken - Ham ...345,000 Bacon - Egg $340,000
WITH	Chicken - Bacon ....348,000 Ham - Egg 350,000
BUTTER	Club Sandwich 350,000
AND SYRUP	

Sandwiches

PLAIN WAFFLE 320,000	Hot Dog ... ...200,000 Chicken t250,000
	Hamburger ... ...250,000 Egg 200,000
	Ham 220,000

Chef's Suggestions

WAFFLE WITH BACON 360,000	Hamburger Steak ...380,000 Ham and Eggs ..$450,000
	Hamburger Steak - Egg 420,000 Bacon and Eggs ... 450,000
	Creamed Chicken Omelette 490,000
MINCED HAM WAFFLE 360,000	Plain Omelette ...370,000 Scrambled Eggs ... 370,000
	Chipped Ham Omelette 450,000

Desserts - Pastries - Bread

HOT CAKES WITH SYRUP OR HONEY 340,000	Assorted Cakes ...$ 65,000 Layer Cake ... ...$
	Buttered Toast (2)... 150,000 Bread (2) Butter (2)
	Chicken Roll..130,000

Beverages

	Coffee, per cup ...120,000 Grade A TT Milk $220,000
	Tea, per cup ... ...110,000 Hot Chocolate per cup 230,000

Jam per portion ... ...$ Butter per portion ... ...$

The front of the menu from the Aristocrat Chocolate Shop. Note that the menu items were printed, but the prices were typed in due to the frequent price changes resulting from inflation.

FROM OUR SODA FOUNTAIN

Root Beer......$190.000

Malted Milk ... ...$ 390.0000

Plain Soda any Flavor 110,000	Ice Cream Soda $365,000
Milk Shakes 380,000	Iced Coffee 250,000
Frosted Coffee 365,000	Coffee Cooler 365,000
Iced Chocolate 330,000	Iced Tea 140,000
Coca Cola 140,000	Plain Ice Cream 280,000
Orange Squash	Orange Juice... ... ...

Tomato Juice $170,000

ICE CREAM SUNDAES

Butter Scotch... 360,000	Caramel Sundae $360,000
Chocolate Shop Special 360,000	Chocolate Fudge Sundae 360,000
Pineapple Sundae... 390,000	Peach Melba Sundae... 390,000
Pride of Shanghai 390,000	Fruit Salad Sundae 390,000
Peach Basket Sundae... 390,000	Chocolate Shop Temptation ... 410,000
Black and White Sundae 360,000	Bakerite Special 410,000
L. B. M. Sundae 4100,000	Country Club Sundae... ... ...,410,000
World Fair 410,000	Jigger Sundae 410,000

Banana Split ... ... $ 410,000

Hazelwood Ice Cream Served at Bakerite Chocolate Shops

BAKERITE FACTORY 1432 SINZA ROAD
TELEPHONE 34238

HOME OF BAKERITE PRODUCTS

OUR OWN BAKERY GOODS SOLD AT THE COUNTER

The back of the menu. Note the large costs in terms of the Yuan.

A one cent piece from pre-war. This and the next three photos illustrate
money printed by the Central Bank of China, pre World War II

A 5-cent piece from pre-war

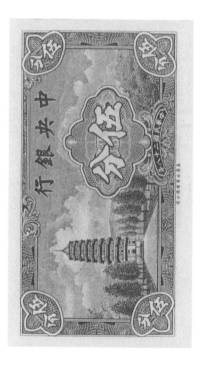

A 5 Yuan note from pre-war

A 10 Yuan note from pre-war

CREDITS

Chapter 1, Beginnings

Shanghai—The Rise and Fall of a Decadent City, by Stella Dong
Strange Haven, by Sigmund Tobias
The Fall of Shanghai, by Noel Barber
Unpublished Jacob Family Tree, by Rose Jacob Horowitz
Conversations with Jack Guri, formerly Jack Goldenberg, Israel, and
    Emma Levy Wachtin, Vancouver, Canada
The definitions of Junk and Sampan were found in the *Oxford English
    dictionary, 2nd Edition, 1989.*

Chapter 2, Early Life in Shanghai

Shanghai—The Rise and Fall of a Decadent City, by Stella Dong
Life and Death in Shanghai, by Nien Cheng
The Rape of Nanking, by Iris Chang
Shanghai Boy, Shanghai Girl, Lives in Parallel, by George Wang and Betty
    Barr
Fourth Marines in China 1927-1941, from www.Shanghai-ed.com,
    provided by Michael Orapello
Photos, articles, magazine supplements from the North China Daily
    News, Aug. —Sept. 1937, provided by Richard Kask
Conversations with Katie Goldenberg Short, and Shulie Nissim
The definition of Tiffin was found in the *Oxford English Dictionary, 2nd
    Edition, 1989.*
The description of the Festival of Purim was found in the Encyclopedia
    Judaica, Encyclopedia Brittanica, and The Interpreter's Dictionary of
    the Bible.

Chapter 3, War
The Battle of Shanghai, by David H. Grover
Strange Haven, by Sigmund Tobias
Shanghai—The Rise and Fall of a Decadent City, by Stella Dong
Secret War in Shanghai, by Bernard Wasserstein
From The Rivers of Babylon To The Whangpoo, by Maisie Meyer
Standard Catalogue of World Paper Money, 2000, ninth edition, General
    Issues,
1368-1960
Conversations with Emma Levy Wachtin and Katie Levy Fox, Katie
    Goldenberg Short, Charlie Stock, and Jackie Levy
The sinking of the Conte Verde was obtained from the website
    http://rickshaw.org/sinking.htm

Chapter 4, Postwar
Shanghai—The Rise and Fall of a Decadent City, by Stella Dong
The Fall of Shanghai, by Noel Barber

Conversations with many people regarding the effects of inflation: Katie
Levy Fox, Charlie Stock, Bobbie Tchakalian, Rahma Levy Thomas, Leah
Jacob Garrick, and others.

Menu from Aristocrat Chocolate Shop provided by Mayna Avent Nance.

Chapter 5, Life Under Communism
Conversations with Rose Jacob Horowitz

BIBLIOGRAPHY

Wang, George and Barr, Betty. *Shanghai Boy Shanghai Girl, Lives in Parallel*, Old China Hand Press, Hong Kong, 2002.

Dong, Stella. *Shanghai The Rise and Fall of a Decadent City*, William Morrow—Harper Collins Publishers, Inc., New York, NY, 2000

Grover, David H. *The Battle of Shanghai—1941*, Western Maritime Press, Napa, CA, 1994

Patent, Gregory. *Shanghai Passage,* Clarion Books, New York, NY, 1990.

Wasserstein, Bernard. *Secret War in Shanghai*, Houghton Miflin Company, New York, NY, 1998.

Tobias, Sigmund. *Strange Haven*, University of Illinois Press, Urbana and Chicago, IL, 1999.

Lee, Leo Ou-Fan. *Shanghai Modern: the Flowering of a New Urban Culture in China, 1930—1945*, Harvard University Press, Cambridge, MA, 1999.

Anecdotes of Old Shanghai, distributed by Shanghai Branch, Shanghai Cultural Publishing House, Shanghai, China, 1985.

Cheng, Nien. *Life and Death in Shanghai*, Grove Press, New York, NY, 1986.

Standard Catalogue of World Paper Money, Volume 2, General Issues, 1368—1960 Krause Publications Iola, WI, 2000.

Chang, Iris. *The Rape of Nanking,* Penguin Books, New York, NY, 1997.

Barber, Noel. *The Fall of Shanghai,* Coward, McCann & Geoghegan, New York, NY, 1979.

National Geographic Magazine, March, 1994, article on Shanghai, pages 2-35.

Meyer, Maisie. *From The Rivers of Babylon To the Whangpoo. A Century of Sephardi Jewish Life in Shanghai.* University Press of America,

Lanham, Maryland, Oxford, UK. 2003

Websites

www. sinomedia.net

www.shanghai-ed.com

www.talesofoldchina.com

www.eh.net/hmit/exchangerate/infoafr.htm

www.chinaculture.org

www.umass.edu/wsp/sinology/persons/reifler.html

www.rickshaw.org/sinking.htm

END NOTES

[1]*Bund* is an Anglo-Indian word of Persian origin, meaning an artificial embankment, dam, dyke or causeway. In Anglo-Chinese ports it meant an embankment or quay along the shore.

[2]This comes from the Chinese. *Sam* means three and *Pan* means board or plank. Three boards were strapped together to form a flat-bottomed boat, no more than 10 feet long. It sometimes had a deck or level above the bottom.

[3]This word probably originated in Java, from the Javanese word djong. The word means a large vessel in the China Seas, flat-bottomed, square prow, prominent stem, full stern, carrying lugsails. It was applied to Chinese, Japanese, Malayan, Javanese and South Indian vessels. It found its way into French (*jongue*), Dutch (*jonk*), and Spanish and Portuguese (*junco*).

[4]See Iris Chang's excellent book *The Rape of Nanking*.

[5]The word *tiffin* comes from the old English slang meaning a sip of a drink or a snack. It mutated to mean a noonday meal or luncheon, and used in the Anglo-Indian vernacular in India and the countries to the east.

[6]See *Life and Death In Shanghai* by Nien Cheng.

[7]The HMS Peterel should have been named the Petrel, but was named the Peterel by mistake due to a typographical error in some correspondence. The name stuck. Page 2 of *The Battle of Shanghai* by David Grover.

[8] From Maisie Meyer's book "From The Rivers of Babylon To the Whangpoo," Page 97.